Scattered

my year as an
accidental caregiver

JANA
PANARITES

Copyrighted Material

Scattered: My Year As An Accidental Caregiver

Copyright © 2015 by Jana Panarites All Rights Reserved.

No part of this publication may be reproduced, stored in a retrieval system or transmitted, in any form or by any means—electronic, mechanical, photocopying, recording or otherwise—without prior written permission from the publisher, except for the inclusion of brief quotations in a review.

For information about this title or to order other books and/or electronic media, contact the publisher:
Agewyz Press
PO Box 16413, Alexandria, VA 22302
www.agewyz.com

ISBNs: 978-0-9964035-0-4 (print)
  978-0-9964035-1-1 (eBook)

Printed in the United States

Cover and Interior design: 1106 Design

    Panarites, Jana.
       Scattered : my year as an accidental caregiver / Jana Panarites.
      pages cm
      ISBN 978-0-9964035-0-4
      ISBN 978-0-9964035-1-1

       1. Panarites, Jana. 2. Panarites, Jana—Family. 3. Women caregivers—United States—Biography. 4. Adult children of aging parents—United States—Biography. 5. Mothers and daughters—United States—Biography. 6. Aging parents—Care—United States. 7. Parent and adult child. I. Title.

HQ1063.6.P36 2015   306.874092
                                    QBI15-600107

For Peter and Helen

Contents

1.	Forty Days	1
2.	Hollywood Ending	57
3.	The Landing	69
4.	The Road of Trials	75
5.	Sold Out	106
6.	The Odd Couple	114
7.	What Do You Do?	121
8.	Go-To Girl	141
9.	Drowning, Not Waving	153
10.	Lights, Cameras, Action	174
11.	The Unbearable Lightness of Tuscany	191
12.	State of Mind	215
13.	You Can Do It	231
14.	The Deluge	243
15.	A Better Place	268
16.	The Escape Hatch	274

1
Forty Days

I'LL NEVER LEAVE YOU. That was the promise my father had made to my mother during their fifty-six years of marriage. I could imagine him saying something like that in a fleeting, chivalrous way. And I could imagine my mother believing him, because Dad was a man of his word. But in our final conversation, it was the sound of my father's voice that I clung to rather than anything he said.

It was the Monday before Thanksgiving 2009, and my parents had just returned to Washington, DC after a weekend in New York City. When they called me in Los Angeles, the first thing I noticed was the lateness of the hour: 11:30 p.m. on the East Coast.

"You guys are still up?"

"Oh, we're just getting started," my father joked in his trademark baritone voice. It was rock solid, like his name in Greek, *Petros,* which translated as "stone."

"How's our California girl?" my mother asked from the extension.

"Not bad," I said, lying to avoid worrying them.

I was close to a nervous breakdown. I had always worked hard, financing my creative projects with all kinds of soul-crushing jobs, at times scraping just to get by. But now I was nearly broke, and without a decent job, at fifty years old. The only saving grace was that I was single and didn't have kids, which meant I was responsible only for myself.

"Tell me about your trip to New York," I said, pacing the parquet floor of my one-bedroom apartment, knowing I was less likely to start crying if we talked about them instead of me.

"It was delightful," my father said. "Great company, perfect weather. New York is gorgeous in the fall."

"We're looking so forward to seeing you at Christmas," said my mother.

"Me too." I faltered. "It's been tough."

"Try not to get discouraged," said my father.

"Well, I'm done with LA." I thought LA was probably done with me, too, given my dire predicament here.

Between the sixteen years I'd lived in New York City, and my two stretches in LA, I had moved eleven times. My father listened patiently as I floated the idea of moving to San Francisco, or Oakland, or Seattle, or Portland. I could work in a vineyard. There were tons of vineyards in the Pacific Northwest. Why not apprentice at a winery? Or, I could move back east.

"Who knows," I said. "Maybe I'll move back to DC."

"We would love that," said my father.

He sounded so happy, which made me feel worse. Never in a million years would I move back to stuffy and political

DC. I only tossed out the possibility because I was desperate to salvage my career, to escape financial ruin, and anywhere but LA seemed a better place to achieve these goals.

"You take care of yourself," my father said.

"Goodnight, Dad. I love you."

"Love you too, dear."

THE NEXT MORNING I was awoken by the sound of knocking on my apartment window. When I opened the back door, my neighbor Greg rushed inside and gripped me by the shoulders.

"Jana," he said. "Your father had a heart attack. He passed away last night."

I felt like I was hit by a freight train.

"Your sisters have been trying to reach you all night. They called me, but I just got the message. I'm so sorry."

"I turned off the phones," I said, my mind spinning, filled with fear.

I had slept through my father's death. I reached for the couch, sobbing, convulsing.

"Oh God…" I had to sit down. But, no—I had to call home. Where was my BlackBerry?

Find it, I thought. *Call Mom.*

Mom without Dad. Me without Dad. Dad was dead?

Dial the number.

My sister Tasha answered the phone at my parents' house. Bits of information dribbled out, but there was no coherent whole. *Fell in the bathroom. 9-1-1. Ambulance.* She told me our sister Zoë was flying in from Florida this afternoon.

"I'll be there tonight," I said.

I packed in a thunderstruck daze.

By the time I completed my cross-country trip, I felt like I hadn't slept in a week. My brother-in-law, George, picked me up at Dulles airport and we shot to the Capital Beltway.

"I'm confused by what happened," I said through tears.

"Apparently your mom got out of bed in the middle of the night because your dad wasn't there and she wondered where he was. She found him on the bathroom floor, bleeding at the temple."

My hands were shaking. *Bleeding at the temple. Dad on the floor.*

"By the time Tasha and I got there, the EMT crew was trying to revive him. We followed the ambulance to the hospital thinking it was a stroke, but when the doctor came into the waiting room she told us he'd had a heart attack and died—just like that."

"Where is he now?"

"At Pumphrey's," said George. "The funeral home."

I felt nauseous, imagining my father lying there on a slab in the basement.

When we arrived at my parents' house in North Bethesda, Maryland, I stared at the red brick Colonial, afraid of what I would find inside. Chilly air seeped into the sleeves of my leather coat as I went to the front entrance. I reached for the knocker, but stopped when I noticed that the door wasn't fully closed.

"Hello?" I pushed inside, squinting in the foyer.

It seemed abnormally dark in the house, as if the electricity had gone out and everyone had resorted to using flashlights. The stillness in the air was terrifying. I moved in, shaken by the sight of my diminutive, flaxen-haired mother standing like an apparition in the hallway. At eighty years old, her looks and energy belied her actual age, but the devastation in her face was something I had never seen in my mother. She seemed to have aged twenty years in less than twenty-four hours.

"Mom."

I embraced her tiny frame. She didn't move, or say anything. As we separated I noticed my father's gold wedding band hanging from her neck, on a thin, gold chain.

"Come inside," my mother whispered.

The recessed lights in the kitchen were dimmed as if for a séance. Glasses of half-consumed wine dotted the marble table. I poured myself a glass of red and joined my mother and sisters. We were four grown women at the family breakfast table: three without a father, and one without a husband.

"Two fifty-six a.m.," my mother said, recalling my father's recorded time of death.

I studied her olive skin, the texture of fine sandpaper, and her wide, high cheekbones that intensified her stoic expression. Between that and her tinted glasses, she reminded me of an elegant, yet doomed Jackie Kennedy.

I felt a heaving in my stomach, and began sobbing.

"Go ahead, dear," said my mother. "I'm done crying. I have no more tears."

I paused, confused. Surely she wasn't done crying?

My sister Tasha explained how the next few days would unfold. The plan for her and my brother-in-law to do Thanksgiving had been scrapped. The holiday was now irrelevant. The wake for my father would be on Friday, with two separate viewings. The funeral service would be Saturday morning, followed by a final prayer at the gravesite. In keeping with our Greek heritage, there would be a memorial luncheon, or *makaria*, afterward where the guests could offer remembrances of my father.

"I already called the club," Tasha said. "They e-mailed me a menu for fifty people."

"The details of death," my mother said.

I studied her pallid face. My mother seemed so detached. I guessed she was in shock.

"It feels like he's still here," I said, shivering.

"I know," said Tasha. "Forty days," she added, as a reminder.

According to the Greek Orthodox Church, my father's physical body had fallen asleep and separated from his soul. His spirit was now wandering the earth, just as Christ had wandered the earth following His death and resurrection. Many Greeks believed this forty-day journey involved visits to people and places the deceased knew during his or her lifetime. The eeriness in our house suggested my father was now on a ghostly farewell tour.

"Two fifty-six a.m.," my mother said again.

I stared at the wedding band hanging from her neck, imagining a mortician removing it from my father's lifeless right hand.

Tasha left to go back to her and George's house, fifteen minutes away, while Zoë and my mother went upstairs to bed. I sat at the breakfast table a moment longer, in a familiar place, but confused by the speed with which I'd gotten there and the frightening reason why. It was still Tuesday, right? I had to get to Saturday. I drained my wine glass, gazing a moment at the square of black night showing through the skylight. My father had installed the cutout to bring the outside indoors. Lowering my head, I thought, *is Dad really gone for good?*

I dreaded the coming days. Pushing away from the table, I headed upstairs.

At the top of the stairs, the closed door on my left took me aback. It was the door to my father's bathroom, outside the master bedroom. I knew he wasn't behind the door. Had my mother kept it closed to avoid reliving the horror of my father's collapse? The room seemed like a No Trespassing zone. Spooked, I latched onto the railing, and made a U-turn down the hallway. At the far end I saw Zoë gazing with trepidation at something behind me. I followed her sight line, to where my mother was peering out of the master bedroom door.

"Would one of you girls sleep with me?" she said in a small voice.

"I will," I said. "I'll be there in a moment."

"Thanks," said Zoë. "I can't do it."

I wasn't eager to sleep in my father's bed, either, but one of us had to answer the call of duty. I changed into some flannel pajamas, washed my face, and went into my parents' bedroom, squeamish. There was only one light on in the room, and it was over the night table on my father's side of the king-sized bed. The sheets on his side were rumpled, as if he were still alive and had just stepped away for a few minutes. I tiptoed to my father's side of the bed, eyeing the satin drapes and familiar Chinese prints above the bed, framed in triplicate on the bamboo wallpaper. Everyday objects unchanged by death. I lay down next to my mother, facing away from her. The sheets were cold, but after a few seconds the urge to make my mother feel safe overwhelmed my discomfort.

I turned out the light and fell onto my father's pillow, imagining him lying there a few hours ago. In my mind I replayed our last conversation, trying to comfort myself with the fact that the last words between us were "I love you."

THE NEXT TWO DAYS melded together as a flood of visitors came to our house with trays of *spanakopita, moussaka,* and all manner of Greek pastries. They sat around the breakfast table sharing their memories of Dad. Throughout the visitations, my mother wept silent tears. It was hard to believe this was the same woman who had so recently asked, "How's our California girl?" in a high-spirited way. And it was hard to believe I could feel worse now than I had in that conversation.

The day before the wake I took my mother to get her nails done.

"My life is over," she said, as we drove to the salon.

"Please don't say that," I said. "You're in good health, and you still have your family. We need you." I paused. "*I* need you."

Back at the house I took calls on my mother's behalf and assisted Tasha with the *details of death*. When I sent her an e-mail saying I'd taken Mom to the nail salon and slept with her on the night of my arrival from LA, Tasha replied, "You are so good to her and for her. Please move back!"

My whole life was on the West Coast. Did my sister really expect me to just up and leave, to be *good to* our mother? I didn't respond. I was too busy thinking about my father. I wasn't convinced he was actually gone for good. The three-day wait while the funeral home prepared his body for the wake only served to fuel my doubts. My father could be anywhere. Maybe he was attending a business conference, or out playing golf with a friend or upstairs paying bills.

THE DAY OF THE WAKE finally arrived. With my mother on one arm, I entered a large, ornate room inside the Pumphrey Funeral Home. My body went taut at the sight of my father's profile, barely visible in a mahogany casket set against the far wall, surrounded by colorful flowers bursting out of vases, and wreaths on easels. The scene was so ghoulish it seemed unreal.

Edging forward toward my father's body, I felt a sharp tug on my arm and stiffened it to prevent my mother from crumpling to the floor. But then she regained her balance and went directly to the casket. She did her *stavro*, the Greek sign of the cross, and stared in disbelief at her husband before kissing him on the cheek. Turning aside, her legs started to buckle.

I rushed in and propped her up, stealing a glance at the man in the coffin, puzzled by what I saw. He didn't look anything like my father, but he was wearing Dad's navy blue Brooks Brothers suit and wire-framed glasses.

"Let's sit down." I guided my mother to a crushed velvet couch.

She began crying. "Oh, Jana, what am I going to do?"

"You'll be okay," I said, doubting my own words, welcoming the mourners who now descended on my mother. I felt anxious for her future and was already worked up about my own. Were my sisters concerned about Mom? Where were they anyway?

I looked up and saw Zoë in a scrum of guests near the entrance. Tasha was talking with someone from the funeral home. Finally she came toward me.

"I'll sit with Mom for a while," said Tasha.

She didn't seem insensitive to my mother's crying, but she didn't seem too concerned by it, either. Maybe I was overreacting.

I got up and let Tasha take my place. Eyes wet, I drifted to my father's side and placed a hand on top of his, flinching at the cold, hard touch. His jowls seemed unnaturally thick and his skin caked with make-up. The cut on his temple, from his fall in the bathroom, had been neatly patched over. My father looked like a wax figure. But this was all I had left of him, so I kissed him on the cheek. The evidence was irrefutable: my father was dead.

THE NEXT DAY I FELT less edgy; I had finally seen my father's body, and had made the connection between the shock of what I'd been told and what I could see for myself. But I still had to get through the funeral service, go back to LA, and sort out my mess of a life. It was Saturday, right? It had to be, because the wake was yesterday and that was the Friday after Thanksgiving, and it was time for the funeral which my sister said would take place on Saturday morning.

You can do this, I thought, inching into the Greek Orthodox Church of St. George with my mother on my arm like a sidecar. In the vestibule were some familiar-looking people: solemn-faced mourners lighting candles, signing the guest book, saying prayers before a glass-covered Christ icon. I had seen them at the wake, or at our house, or both. Their ongoing presence calmed me.

The priest—a tall, bearded man with a youthful demeanor despite being middle-aged—greeted our family. Calm until this point, at the sight of him my mother began crying again.

"I know," said the priest, hugging her. "It's awful. But his life isn't over."

His words threw me. My father had died. His life was over for me.

"Can we go in?" said my mother under her breath.

I nodded, shuffling forward, stopping as my mother prayed before a Christ icon. The image of a Byzantine saint on the face of a laminated prayer card caught my eye. I took the card out of its jar and examined the back of it, fixated on the words, *In Loving Memory of Peter E. Panarites. April 24, 1930–November 24, 2009.* Beneath were the words, *Miss Me But Let Me Go.* Moved, I showed the card to my mother. She cupped her mouth, shaking her head.

I put my arm around her. We went into the church proper, up the center aisle. The choir was chanting over organ music: "Ahh-gheeeee-os… ahh-gheeeee-os." I felt like I was slumming on sacred ground. I rarely went to church, let alone this one three thousand miles away from LA.

I took in the stained glass windows, the rows of auburn wooden pews and the ivory, pitched roof with intersecting, pinewood beams. Close to the altar was a mosaic dome with a Christ figure in the center, looking down on everyone with open arms, and an undercurrent of pity that made me feel less significant than I already felt.

Ahead I saw my father in his open casket. I felt sad and a little uncomfortable. It seemed like we were following his dead body everywhere, as if my father were a traveling exhibition. I slipped into a pew and sat next to my mother. In my head I heard the sound of my father's voice: "Delightful… perfect weather. New York is gorgeous in the fall." I wished I were anywhere but here.

The priest appeared in a gold-and-white brocaded robe. Facing the screen of icons at the back of the sanctuary, he did his *stavro*, and called out in a rhythmic voice: "To the Father and the Son and the Holy Spirit, now and forever and to the ages of ages."

The choir behind me sang, "Amen." They sang a funeral dirge as the priest chanted in Greek and in English: "Dear Lord, we ask that you give rest to the soul of the departed Peter Panarites, and forgive all his sins."

I stared at my father's coffin, the sharp odor of incense filling my nose as the deacon circled the casket, swinging a chain of bells back and forth like a pendulum. Clouds of smoke filled the air. The odor and the bells brought me back to the church services of my youth, soothing me now.

The priest faced the congregation, reciting the scriptures and prayers of absolution in a speak-song cadence, alternating between Greek and English. I lost track of the passage of time, distracted by my father in his coffin, but soon I heard the priest speaking in English only: "Through the prayers of our Holy Fathers, Lord Jesus Christ, have mercy and save us." The choir chanted, "Amen."

"We are here to give thanks," said the priest, "for the life of the dearly departed Peter Panarites... loving father to three daughters, dear husband to his wife, Helen... friend, colleague or relative to everyone here. Although he is gone from the earth and we feel his loss deeply, we draw strength from the knowledge that Peter is now asleep in the hands of the Lord, preparing for a new life with God."

It seemed odd that the priest was talking about my father, who rejected any notion of an afterlife. "This is it," he had said many times. I could still see my father tapping the table, saying "It all happens here." I felt the same way. But as I listened to the priest, I wanted to believe my father and I were wrong and that Dad was alive somewhere, maybe in a distant world. Because he loved being alive, and I didn't want it to be over for him yet.

The priest reminded us all of the frailty of human life, and emphasized the importance of leading a purposeful life given its brevity. I lowered my head. My own life was anything but purposeful. I felt utterly directionless. I let out a long breath as the priest encouraged people to come forward to say a final farewell to my father.

I made my way to his body, kissing my father for the last time, though I felt he was long gone. "I love you," I whispered.

My mother approached the coffin and stared at my father for a moment. She kissed him and quickly came toward me as if she couldn't bear to look at him any longer.

I helped her down the altar steps. As we walked down the crimson carpet, I saw for the first time that the pews were completely packed. There must have been three hundred people in the church. A collective gaze followed my mother and me as we exited the church. It was startling, and surreal. I was overwhelmed by the show of support.

Outside, the sun had come out; it had turned into a beautiful, late autumn day. But the hearse at the curb stood out like a crow on a snowy plain. As the driver swung open the back door, I winced at the creamy interior and steered my mother toward the parking lot.

Zoë appeared from behind with my mother's only sibling, whom we called Thea, the Greek word for aunt. She was a spunky, eighty-three-year-old divorcée who lived on her own in DC. Without a word, we all climbed into my mother's old Mercedes. I started the car and it shook with ferocity, as if choking on a bone.

"It was a lovely service," my aunt said. "Didn't you think so, Helen?"

I glanced at my unresponsive mother in the rearview mirror. Her head was tilted back and I assumed her eyes were closed, but I couldn't see them behind her tinted eyeglasses. Unsettled by her remoteness, I backed out and drove slowly to the front of the church.

I pulled up behind the hearse, waiting as a stream of mourners came out of the chapel, followed by relatives carrying the casket. A chill came over me at the thought that my father was locked away for good.

The driver of the hearse approached the car, looking as if he needed to speak with me. I lowered my window. "We're taking the long way to the cemetery," he said. "And, I'll be driving slowly, so put on your flashers."

I nodded distractedly, grateful for his guidance, and triggered the hazard lights.

Soon the hearse began moving. I followed the black car, turning onto a two-lane road with the lanes going in opposite directions. I kept a distance of about three car lengths behind the hearse, deep in thought as I imagined my father *asleep* in the car ahead of me. I felt close to him, and was glad to be near him, to say my long goodbye.

The road widened and I caught a flash of movement on my left. It was my brother-in-law, George, gunning his car past mine.

"Shit—" I slowed as he turned sharply in front of me, settling in behind the hearse. I was stunned. I knew George could be a jerk, but I hadn't experienced this side of him in a while, living in LA all these years. Somehow it didn't seem appropriate to lean on the horn during a funeral procession. I drove on in silence, my anger sapped by grief. So much for my long goodbye.

When we arrived at the Gate of Heaven Cemetery, I parked on the roundabout near the hearse and got out of the car. I felt worn out and was eager for the final blessing at the gravesite to be over. My father's casket was being carried up a grassy incline, to a tented area. At the back of the tent were two men in military uniform. I remembered George had arranged for the full-dress, color guard unit. Like my father, he'd had a brief stint in the Air Force, and he wanted Dad to be honored for his service. That was the thing about George: he could be really thoughtful. But he could also be a jerk.

"Take my arm," I said to my mother as she stepped out of the car. Silently she latched onto me and let me guide her to the tent.

We sat along the edge of the tent in foldout chairs, inches away from the flag-draped coffin. My mother managed to contain her sobbing as the sound of "Taps" filled the air, but then, when I placed an arm around her shoulders, her body began convulsing and she began weeping. I exhaled, wiping my own wet eyes, crying for her sorrow—and mine.

The bugle went silent and the men in uniform removed the American flag from my father's coffin. They folded it into a perfect tri-corner pillow, and then one of the soldiers—an earnest-looking black youth no more than eighteen years old—knelt before my mother and presented her with the folded flag. He gazed in her direction, but not directly at her. A tear streamed down the soldier's face. My mother stopped crying and her body went still. She raised her right hand, and gently wiped away the young man's tear. I watched in amazement; this was the mother I was more familiar with—the tower of strength, able to set aside her pain to console someone else.

The deacon gave the final blessing, showering my father's casket with drops of water, flung from a perforated urn shaped like an ice cream cone. When it was over, I kissed the casket, and moved aside. My mother kissed her gloved hand and pressed it against the coffin. She slipped the *Miss Me But Let Me Go* prayer card through the slit in the middle, turned away, and fell against me for support. We moved down the grassy incline, all but stumbling toward the car.

WHEN WE ARRIVED AT THE CLUB for the *makaria* luncheon, I followed Zoë and my mother into a high-ceilinged ballroom. It was lavish, with crystal chandeliers and cloth-covered tables. It took me a moment to absorb the old guard setting. It seemed far removed from my pared-down urban life.

My parents had joined Congressional Country Club when I was a junior in college, so it wasn't part of my upbringing.

I don't mean to suggest that I didn't have certain privileges growing up—Mom and Dad loved to travel, and took us to Bermuda and Greece as children—but I went to public schools and had paying jobs during the summers. Joining a country club was the furthest thing from my mind. But I understood why my father aspired to it: as the son of Greek immigrants, becoming a member was a mark of achievement. Still, when they first brought me to the club, I chafed at its plantation-style entrance and the de facto Talbot's dress code. I teased my parents, saying they were no longer Greeks. Now they were WASPy Greeks who preferred to downplay their roots.

Entering the ballroom now, I felt like I was in another dimension, thrown by the setting and the throng of people. I had exchanged bits of information about my father with most everyone in the room, but now I could barely recall anything said.

I felt my mother brush past me and cut to a table near the front of the room. She sat down and bowed her head, as if praying to be left alone. I studied her, unused to seeing my mother so withdrawn. I reminded myself that it was natural under the circumstances, and set my sights on the bar across the room.

Moving toward the bar, I thought, *Dad's history is in this room.* The energy in the room was familiar, but I couldn't pinpoint it because I felt like I was floating through a dream. I kept thinking my father would somehow arrive and launch into one of his eloquent, impromptu speeches. But then I remembered he wasn't going to show up, and I worked out that the energy in the ballroom was the same as it had been at the wrap parties I'd attended at the end of every grueling television production I'd ever worked on during my career in entertainment. By the time the party rolled around, the communal suffering had been so great, the crew felt like family. I realized the thread that connected everyone in the ballroom was the suffering we had endured together in the last five days.

I took a glass of wine from the bar and slipped back into the crowd, experiencing a jumble of emotions as I sidled up to my cousin, Nick. He was in his midsixties, from my mother's side of the family in Toronto. During my childhood visits he took me for nighttime motorcycle rides in my pajamas.

"Hey," Nick said. "How are you holding up?"

"Better, now that the funeral is over." I scanned the room, spacey, drink in hand.

Out of the corner of my eye I saw Nick's mouth moving, but I didn't register any sound. I snapped to attention. "I'm sorry. What did you say?"

"It's a nice showing of people." Nick paused. "What are you thinking?"

"That if I moved here, I would become like this."

"Huh…?"

"Status quo," I said. "You know, part of the establishment."

Nick looked at me like I had two heads. "You would be *you*," he said.

A piercing sadness came over me. I realized I had completely lost my sense of self. The quirky middle child who used to be me had disappeared and gone AWOL. That person never would have worried about being sucked into a status quo vortex; she was "the creative one" in the family, the adventurer who had moved to LA from New York at age forty-three. I had spent my entire adult life in those two cities, ping-ponging from television production work and menial temp jobs, to slogging away as a paralegal while I developed my craft as a writer of film and television scripts, and even a few short stories. It was a constant uphill climb, but I never doubted my chosen path. But, then, after earning a master's degree at age forty-nine, I couldn't land a job. I became so desperate to produce an income, I started pitching anti-aging products. And now the death of my father had left me feeling more rudderless than ever. But Nick seemed to have faith in me, even if I didn't.

He sipped at his scotch. "Shall we sit?"

Deep in thought, I followed my cousin to a table near a floor-to-ceiling window. A hush came over the crowd. Everyone was seated. I turned my chair around to get a better view of the front of the room, where a uniformed wait staff stood at the ready, behind a long buffet table lined with chafing dishes. *I've done that job*, I thought. *Maybe I should just go back to waiting tables.* I took a long drink of wine and sat up, straining to get a glimpse of my mother. She was small to begin with, but with her head bowed all I could see was her hair.

Tasha approached the front of the ballroom to address the crowd. "I want to thank everyone for coming," she said. "And, for all your support during this past week. It's meant so much to our family. My husband George has prepared a short speech, and so has our cousin Nick."

George stood up, clearing his throat. He hesitated, cleared his throat again, and then gazed at the paper shaking in his hand.

"My own father died when I was seventeen," he said, "so I didn't have a father for a long time after that. Then when Tasha and I got engaged—" His voice started to crack. "I began calling her father *Dad* right away."

He gestured out the window. "We played many rounds of golf out there. I'll miss him."

George sat down. *Is that it?* I thought, looking around. It seemed he had lost his nerve and had cut a whole passage out of his speech. In a moment Nick stood up, fortifying himself with a belt of scotch. He seemed much less composed than a few minutes ago. His wife had died recently of cancer, after a long illness; our gathering must have brought back the pain of her death all over again. Nick unfolded a flimsy piece of paper and somehow gave a speech, recalling my father as a classy guy who lured my mother's entire side of the family from Toronto to the DC area.

After Nick sat down, the ballroom went silent for what seemed like an eternity. I looked around, restless.

Tasha popped up from her chair. "As many of you know," she said with an awkward smile, "the *makaria* is a time for sharing memories, so if anyone would like to give a remembrance of our father, please feel free to do so."

She settled back into her chair. The silence resumed. Why wasn't anyone standing up? The ballroom was filled with lawyers. They weren't known for being shy. Frustrated, I thought, *Dad would want us to celebrate his life, not wallow in misery at his passing.*

I sprang out of my chair to the front of the ballroom, and faced the riveted crowd.

"I also want to thank everyone for coming," I said, seized by an inexplicable self-confidence, energized by the crowd and the alcohol in my bloodstream.

"In the last few days, many of you have told me that my father enriched your life. But I'm sure he would say that everyone in this room enriched *his* life."

I felt my voice getting stronger. "Dad had a pretty healthy ego, but he was also humble, and when he met my mother I think he knew he'd met his match."

I glanced at my mother, feeling a flash of depression at her hanging head.

"They both had a sense of adventure," I said, forging ahead, "and it was infectious, something I definitely felt as a child. My parents took us on all kinds of fun vacations, but they also had their own time together, which is probably why their relationship lasted so long. Dad was always supportive of us daughters, no matter what path we chose in our lives." I paused, self-conscious, thinking about how far off the rails I'd gone because of my choices.

Quickly, I recovered. "I felt lucky to have had him for fifty years."

It hit me that I was publicly referring to my father in the past tense. I realized I was past the shock of his death, and had moved on to a place of acceptance.

"And, even though our family is devastated," I said, stammering, "I know, eventually we'll be okay. That's all I have to say. Thank you."

I shot back to my chair, eyeing Zoë, who gave me a sweet smile. I reached for my wine. Soon a young colleague of my father stood and told a funny story about Dad, and the tributes piled up as others stood to speak. I felt a tiny sense of accomplishment for steering the mood in a lighter direction, a flicker of a feeling that I hadn't felt in ages.

LATER THAT EVENING, my aunt and a friend of my mother's from Toronto came to the house for dinner. I welcomed their company, but felt scattered emotionally, unsure of my next move. I went to bed a bundle of nerves, a sensation that carried over to the next day.

It was the day after my father's funeral, and my sisters and I had to go through the grim process of reviewing the papers in his den. Bills had to be paid, accounts closed. As I was heading upstairs, I heard Tasha on the phone in the den. "I do have a copy of his death certificate… yes, I'm the executor." It sounded like she was filing a life insurance claim.

At the top of the landing, my mother cut into my field of vision.

"Mom?" I walked into her bedroom, distressed at her ransacking the dresser drawers, flinging open her teak jewelry boxes. "What are you doing?"

"Looking for your father's wedding band," she said. "I can't find it."

"Did you look in your bathroom?"

"It's not in there. Oh, Jana—I lost his wedding band!"

"We'll find it," I said, my pulse quickening. "Did you look under the bed?"

I dropped to the floor. "I see it!" I scooped out the wedding band and gold chain, and scrambled to my feet. "Here it is."

"Thank God," said my mother, her shoulders settling in relief.

"Turn around." I draped the necklace around her and clasped it shut. My mother faced me, pressing her hand against the gold band.

"Oh, Jana," she said, "I feel so sad."

"I know." I gave her a hug, feeling blue myself.

"What's going to happen to me?"

"You're going to go on living," I said. "And we're going to help you. All of us."

"But I can't do it," said my mother.

"Yes, you can. Don't think too far ahead."

"I need to lie down," my mother said, veering sideways.

"That sounds like a good idea. I'll be next door. Later on we'll all have dinner together."

My mother nodded. I backed out and closed her door, trembling with concern. Her grief seemed so debilitating. How could I go back to LA? I wouldn't be able to function very well, knowing my mother wasn't functioning well at all. But I didn't want to stay here, either. I thought, *you don't have to decide anything now.*

"Jana." My mother poked her head out of her bedroom doorway. "Would you write an obituary?"

I stopped. "There was one in the *Post*. Didn't you see it?"

"I can't remember," said my mother. "But you could write something for the *Herald*."

She meant *The National Herald*, a newspaper aimed at the Greek-American community. My mother had written many articles for the paper, although she'd only once been paid for her work when I convinced her to press the editor for payment, thinking he was taking advantage of her skills. When she told me she didn't mind not being paid, it highlighted our difference as writers; whereas I sought to profit from my work—pitching original screenplays and television shows—for my mother, writing was more of a hobby. I hoped she would get back to it soon.

"Why don't we write it together?" I said, hitting on an idea.

"I don't have the strength," said my mother. "But I know you do."

I didn't say anything. I had never written an obituary, much less one for a family member. A staff member had written the piece in the *Washington Post*. But maybe I could write something for the *Herald* that was more of a remembrance of my father.

"I'll give it a try," I said to my mother.

"Thank you." She wiped her eyes and closed her bedroom door.

I went into the den and sat on the Scandinavian couch, eyeing Tasha still on the phone. Zoë looked up from her pile of papers.

"Is Mom okay?" she said.

"Not really." I told her about the lost and found wedding ring. "I don't know how she's going to get by without him."

"They did everything together," said Zoë.

I reached into a box of my father's legal briefs and gazed at his twisty, confident handwriting. The marked-up briefs that would never be in final form.

AFTER DINNER THAT NIGHT, I stood before the baby grand piano and wondered when I would feel up to "tickling the ivories," as my mother called it. I played the piano by ear, mostly jazz improvisation, but I hadn't sat at this keyboard in ages, and my father's death had taken all the joy out of my heart for doing so now. I placed a finger on B flat, without pressing it down.

Tasha circled around the back of the piano and closed the shutters along the wall.

"Please stay," she said. And then, as if exasperated, she added, "It's time for you to come home."

I drew back, stung by her strict tone. "I can't make that decision now," I said, knowing that saying much more would lead to an argument, which I wasn't in the mood for.

"I can introduce you to my friend Callie," said my sister, in a lighter tone. "She works in marketing and PR. She's funny and irreverent, like you. You guys could work together."

"Doing what?"

"I don't know. You're the creative one. You'll figure it out." As if to seal the deal, she added, "She's from LA!"

I gave her a sour look. "I really don't want to talk about this now."

And with that my sister left. I knew she meant well, but I didn't like being told what to do, much less the suggestion that I'd led a reckless life. *It's time for you to come home.* What the fuck?

It wasn't until I crawled into bed that night that I had the capacity to think objectively about my sister's words. Staring at the ceiling, I thought, *maybe she's right… maybe now was the right time to come home.* Not because I was a reprobate, but because there wasn't much left for me in LA. And I had no desire to go back to New York. Those were the cities that had shaped my identity. But after my father's death, I felt disconnected from them both. I rolled onto my side, anguished. I didn't know where I belonged anymore. The only thing I knew for certain was that I couldn't go on living in a perpetual state of anxiety.

I RODE OUT THE NEXT TWO DAYS, weeping with my mother and sisters, growing tired of my indecision. Eight days had passed since my father's death. I had to figure out the next stage of my life.

I could do it if I went for a walk. The open air calmed my nerves and helped me think clearly.

I went upstairs to my bedroom, to get a sweatshirt from the white wicker dresser. It was filled with old sweaters and pajamas, the last remaining survivors of decluttering initiatives going back to the seventies. I had shared the room with Zoë when we were kids, and the entire bedroom was virtually unchanged from that era, but for the replacement of the twin beds with a king-sized bed notched to a white wicker headboard. Tying together the theme was a white wicker night table. The sight of so much yesteryear furniture made me weak in the knees, conjuring up a past I couldn't fully recall because too many decades had gone by. I couldn't recall the past, and I couldn't see my future. I felt emotionally suspended between two depressingly fuzzy eras.

Hands shaking, I grabbed a sweatshirt from the dresser, threw it on, and went back downstairs. I put on a scarf and gloves found in the hall closet, my father's beige quilted jacket, and his red-and-blue knit cap with the Cornell logo stitched on the front. It felt good to wear some of his clothes, as if part of my father was with me. All bundled up, I went out the front door.

Cold air struck my face as I started down the red brick walkway that led to the street. At the end of the walkway, I turned around to size up my childhood home, as if to challenge its very existence. We had moved into the four-bedroom house in 1971, when I was eleven years old. By now it was a member of our family, like a glamorous movie location that becomes a character itself in the film. But that didn't mean I should return to the location and play the lead role in the script.

Shifting my stance, I began cataloguing the neglected spots of the house: the gutter clogged with leaves, and the ivy on the flagstone wall, sprawling out of control. I stared at the shutterless windows, imagining my mother floating from one empty room to the next, all alone, with no one to talk to after I left for California. I told myself she could pick up the phone and call her friends. Tasha and George would stop by, and so would my aunt. My mother wouldn't be alone. But in the end she would be, wouldn't she? Eventually, they would leave.

I spun off the curb and circled the roundabout, the woodsy odor of burning fireplaces filling my nostrils. I marched down the street, studying the split-level houses, homing in on a modest Colonial. *I wonder if the Brays still live there*, I thought, remembering their kid, Mike, a star baseball player from middle school onward. They must have moved away. Who lived on this street now? I only knew the Kuchners, who lived next door to my parents; they were the longest-running family on the block, my parents being in second place. *The stalwarts*, I thought, unable to wrap my head around the concept of living in one place for four decades.

At the bottom of the street, I turned onto the sidewalk and studied the Cape Cods and Colonials across the street and set back on sloping lawns. The one thing they all had in common was that the lawns were well-maintained. By whom it was anyone's guess, since the neighborhood appeared deserted. I tugged miserably at my sleeves, nearing the elementary school I had attended as a child. The brick box of a school had been bulldozed on one side. A sign on the grounds read: "Closed for Renovations, Re-Opening August 2010." I imagined the halls of the school abuzz with shrieking little voices in less than a year's time. My eyes welled with tears. Where would I be in August 2010? Back in LA, eking out a living? Here in suburbia, surrounded by death? *Keep walking,* I told myself. *Put one foot in front of the other.* Step. Step. Step.

My mind drifted back to the last conversation I'd had with my father, and my claim to be done with LA. Why was I even living there anymore? I hardly ever saw my friends; everyone was always traveling or consumed with work. We were all overachievers, but I was sure I was the only one who felt like a failure. I remembered the joy in my father's voice when I said I might move back to DC. And the guilt I felt instantly at the thought of letting him down. *But why shouldn't I move back?* I thought, daring myself to defy my own prejudices.

And then the significance of that last conversation with my father hit me, and it seemed like the pieces of my shattered life all came together. I realized the conversation wasn't about fulfilling my father's wish for me to move back home—of course he would have been joyful at the possibility, but that didn't mean he expected me to do it. It was about the fact that from Day One my father had never pressured me into living anywhere. After graduating from the University of Vermont, I had voluntarily returned to the DC area, and made the break for California soon afterward, determined to use my writing skills in the film industry.

"I'm leaving DC," I told my father back then.

"Are you staying in the country?" he said.

"Go for it," he seemed to be saying. "Follow your heart." Now that heart was telling me to come home, because that was where I was needed. And I needed a break from my chaotic life. I had no reason to go back to LA, but I had a reason to stay here: my mother needed me, and I needed her.

I HURRIED BACK TO THE HOUSE, filled with a sense of purpose. I sat at the teak desk in my father's den and powered up his laptop. The computer screen lit up with a *ping!* and I leaned into it. I figured I would need about three weeks to close out my life in LA. Should I ship my furniture, or sell it? Having moved so many times, I had learned to live like a monk. I decided that when I got back to LA, I would sell most of my possessions on Craigslist. I would keep the essentials, ship what I couldn't fit in my car, and drive myself east.

I logged onto Orbitz. On the flight reservations page I chose the One-Way option and typed in the airport code for Dulles. I clicked on the grid under the "Leave" field. A December 2009 calendar popped up. My father's forty-day memorial service would take place on Sunday, January 3, 2010. I would stay in Maryland until then and leave for LA the next day.

That settled it. I would fly back to LA on January 4, pack up, and drive back east three weeks later. I felt my anxiety spiking. I rubbed my eyes, telling myself I could always move back to LA—California would always be there. Mom, on the other hand, could fall to pieces and die of a broken heart. In long marriages like hers, it wasn't uncommon for the surviving spouse to lose the will to live. I couldn't lose both parents back to back: that would be unbearable.

Give yourself a year, I thought. *See where things stand after that.* A year wasn't that long. I needed the time to put my life back together.

I narrowed my eyes on the computer screen; the cheerleader in me was back on board, waving pompoms in my head. I told myself it would be easier to rebuild my life here than in LA, because here I would have more resources: namely, a family with connections. And moving in with my mother would give me some breathing room financially. She would never take any money from me (and would be insulted if I offered it), which meant I wouldn't be sweating out each day wondering how I would pay my bills. Of course my mother was grief-stricken, but she seemed healthy and no doubt would return to her life in due course. Living with her would buy me some time; I could use this opportunity to focus on rebuilding my writing career. Then, in a year, we could sell the house and everyone would move on.

For the first time in a long time I felt as if I had a solid plan to build on.

I FELT HOPEFUL ABOUT MY FUTURE. My father was gone, but I was still here, and I wanted to make the most of every day. Maybe I could throw myself into a writing or producing project. Why not bring a little Hollywood pizzazz to the DC area? But it would be silly to throw away the business skills I'd worked so hard to attain, selling those anti-aging products. Could I create *and* sell? *Slow down*, I thought, *first things first.*

I corralled my sisters and mother into the family room to share my life-changing news. I wanted to speak with them as a whole, before Zoë flew back to Florida. She was single, like me, but unlike me she had a job to go back to as an attorney in West Palm Beach.

Planting myself on the long, navy couch, I gazed at my mother seated on the adjacent two-seater. Her eyes were uncertain, but there was tranquility in them, too, as if she had transitioned to a pure state of being, and now saw the world with total clarity.

"I've been thinking a lot about what's happened," I said, "and… well, I've decided to move back."

"Oh, Jana," Tasha gasped. "Yay!" She threw her arms around me, genuinely happy.

I grabbed at the couch to steady myself. When Tasha let go of me, I turned to my mother.

"It's going to be hard," I said, "but"—and that was where I lost it, tears filling my eyes—"I don't want you to go through this alone. Maybe it can be a new beginning for both of us."

My mother gave me a tender smile.

"Now you can come visit me in Florida all the time," Zoë cried. "Both you *and* Mom!"

"Well… not any time soon," I said. "I've got to get my life back on track. And it won't be easy because I'll be helping Mom, too." I paused. "This is a huge change for me," I added with emphasis. "But I'm willing to live in the house for a year. My plan is to fly back to LA in the new year—the day after Dad's memorial service—close up my apartment and drive back to DC. The whole thing shouldn't take more than three weeks."

"The best part is, I didn't push you into it," said my mother. "You made the decision all on your own."

Noticing the look of relief on my sisters' faces, I started to get cold feet. By offering to move home and take care of Mom, was I getting myself into something I wasn't prepared for? Was I not grasping the whole story here? I told myself that whatever I was getting myself into, a year wasn't that long, and I was used to high-pressure situations from working in television production and at hard-charging law firms.

"I'm going upstairs to lie down," said my mother, giving me a hug. "I'm so glad you're staying. If you need money, let me know. Money is the last thing you should worry about."

But I worry about it all the time, I thought, watching her leave the room.

When she was gone, I said to my sisters, "You guys have to stay connected. Zoë is limited by being in Florida, but Tasha, you have to come by and spend time with Mom."

"Of course," she said. "I'll come by on the weekends, and stay with her when you're in California, take her to doctor appointments, whatever she needs."

"That will be good," I said.

"I'll be here for at least a week during Christmas," said Zoë. "Maybe longer."

"That will be good, too."

A DAY LATER, Zoë went back to Florida, and I was alone in the house with my mother for the first time since my father's death. The house seemed bigger without my sisters around, and gloomier, too, all the more so because my mother kept to her bed much of the day. I wondered if she'd started reading the book about grief that my uncle's wife had sent her. So far, I'd only seen her study the cover of the book and set it aside. I wondered how long my mother's inertia would last. Did I have the strength to tough it out? *Quit stewing*, I admonished myself. *Start planning your move.*

I went into the den and sat at my father's desk, my eyes achy from too little sleep. Powering up the computer, I filled out a change of address form online, and e-mailed my landlord in LA to let him know I would be vacating my apartment by the third week of January.

I needed to make some notes. I opened the top left drawer of the desk, jolted by the words "From the Desk of Peter E. Panarites" stenciled atop a white notepad. I felt short of breath, watery-eyed as I removed the pad from the drawer. I realized I hadn't yet started the obituary my mother had asked me to write, which I saw as more of a remembrance. The moving project could wait; I put it aside and began drafting my piece for the *Herald*.

Weeping on and off, I reconstructed the facts of my father's life, from his beginnings in East Rochester to his end in North Bethesda. I wrote about how my father was thrust into running a restaurant with his immigrant mother at age eleven, when his own father died. And about the vats of melted chocolate in the restaurant's back room, how the sweet-smelling goop had sparked my father's lifelong love of chocolate—and given rise to the two-foot tall, solid chocolate Easter bunnies I'd received in my childhood. Year after year I chipped away at those brown bunnies, starting with the ears, working my way down to the feet.

I wrote about my father's long-distance courtship of my mother, their marriage in 1953, and Dad's education at Cornell and then Georgetown law school—though he had dreamt of becoming an architect. We had spoken about this dream when I was in my midthirties.

"Why didn't you become an architect?" I asked my father, wishing he had. Designing buildings seemed much more romantic than being a lawyer.

"Because I knew I wouldn't make any money," said my father. "And we were starting a family, and I had mouths to feed."

Mr. Responsible: that was my father. I showcased his sense of humor, writing about how my father had come up with a name for an organization comprised of Greek-American lawyers living in the DC area. At the luncheon after the funeral one of the lawyers had explained Dad's rationale behind his chosen name: Hellenic American Lawyers International Association.

"Look at the initials," my father argued. "H.A.L.I.A." In Greek, the word *halia* means *mess*. It was so typical of my father to find a solution using humor.

I paid tribute to his love of culture, reminded of how Dad had given us daughters an opera or jazz CD every year at Christmas.

"I think you'll like that," I remember him saying, as I opened a Dexter Gordon CD.

"There's more than one." I flipped to the one beneath it: *The Magnificent Thad Jones*.

My father's eyes twinkled. "I thought you'd like to build up your collection."

He loved being the provider on many levels; music was no exception. Most everything I knew of jazz, I owed to my father. I wrote of his love of spending time together as a family, recalling the trip to Greece he had orchestrated in 1972 so we could experience our roots firsthand, and of how my father had spearheaded a trip to the Greek island of Andros, where we assembled as adults. Elegant, smart, and generous. That was my father.

Writing his remembrance was painful, but it helped me in my grief. The process seemed to bring us closer together, and I discovered certain patterns in my father's life that explained a few patterns in my own: the instinct to help his widowed mother run the restaurant was similar to my instinct to help my widowed mother. I realized my father and I were both dreamers, and that, in a way—for better or worse—in choosing the creative life, I had fulfilled his dream of becoming an architect. I thought if we were that much alike, maybe my father knew all along that I would come home, because that was the responsible thing to do: to take care of Mom and me, and keep the family intact. My father had done that for so long. Now it was my turn.

It was pitch black outside by the time I finished writing the remembrance, but I felt satisfied at completing the work. I tiptoed into my mother's cave-like bedroom, and stood over her, an immobile lump under a red-and-black Hudson Bay blanket. *When she dies*, I mused, *I'll be the one to find her, and this is how she'll look.* Why did I have to think that just then? I was unnerved at how often such macabre notions had flashed through my mind since my father's death.

"Mom," I whispered. "I'm going to heat up some dinner."

She rolled over, her eyes cracking open like an egg hatching a chick. "I'm not hungry."

"We'll wait an hour, and then eat," I said. "You have to get some food into your system."

I felt disoriented. I had never addressed my mother so sternly, as if she were a child. Standing a little wobbly, I moved toward the closet as if pulled by the force of gravity.

I opened the lemon-colored door, gazing at my father's suits and ties hanging before me. Everything was so well organized, oozing Dad's persona. I flipped on the automated tie rack, entranced by the motorized efficiency as the rack looped clockwise. I turned off the power, realizing I hadn't asked my mother what she wanted to do with my father's clothes. I'd been avoiding the subject as if it were off limits, like the "No Trespassing" zone of my father's bathroom. Maybe my mother wanted to hold onto his clothes for a while and clutch at them behind closed doors.

"Mom," I called out, "Should we give Dad's clothes to Goodwill?"

"I don't care what you do with them," she said. "Just take everything away."

Her response shook me, but then I remembered my mother's pragmatic nature.

"Or, maybe George wants them," said my mother.

"Wouldn't that be hard for you… to see him wearing Dad's clothes?"

"It doesn't matter," said my mother. "Ask him."

I called Tasha from the den. On my father's desk was an egg-shaped, alabaster paperweight, with the scales of justice etched on its face. I picked up the heavy object.

"Hey, it's me," I said, when my sister answered the phone sniffling. "Are you okay?"

"I guess so," said Tasha. "I was just having a cry… thinking about Dad."

"I've been weepy, myself. Mom wants me to ask if George wants Dad's suits and ties."

"That's weird." Tasha hesitated. "Well, I'm sure he'd love to have them. How are you guys doing over there?"

"Mom's sleeping," I said, "and has been all day."

"She's depressed," said Tasha. "It's natural. But she should see her doctor, just to check in."

"I was thinking the same thing. Dr. Post, right?"

"Yes," said Tasha.

"I'll make the appointment."

"Thanks. And I'll get Dad's clothes, when I come over to look at the bills." Tasha was handling the finances, the ongoing *details of death*.

We said our goodbyes. I stared at the paperweight, clutched in my hand.

PLODDING DETERMINEDLY through December, I continued to fill in the days before flying back to LA, with an eye to maintaining my mother's health. I didn't have much else to do, and given her heartache and older age, it seemed like a slippery slope from depression to bodily decay. Each morning before going out for a walk, I set out my mother's rack of pills in the middle of the kitchen counter alongside a glass of water. She went straight to them, and gulped down the pills. I was happy when my mother starting eating again and even preparing her own food. But there were signs of trouble ahead, even as she made progress in attending to her own needs.

Late one morning when I was going through a pile of condolence cards, I saw my mother remove a pot of hot water from the stove, spoon out the boiled egg, and come toward me with her breakfast.

"Mom," I said, eyeing the flaming red disc on the range, "you forgot to turn off the stove."

She set down her plate with a dead-eyed gaze. "Oh." She went back to the stove, clicked the knob counterclockwise.

Two days later, I came into the kitchen to find my mother sitting at the table in front of a plate of English muffin and Canadian bacon. The partially opened oven door caught my eye, and as I looked inside, I saw the broiler coils were apricot yellow.

"Mom," I sighed, "you left the oven on." I flicked it off.

"Could you turn it off?" she said in a flat voice.

"I did." I stood next to her. "Please be more careful."

She nodded vacantly and cut into her bacon, in tiny labored movements.

I assumed my mother's absent-minded behavior was a byproduct of grief, but what if it persisted while I was in LA? To hedge my bets (and hopefully prevent her from burning the house down), I made a sign that read "Turn Oven Off," and taped it next to the appliance. I did the same with the stove, like I was childproofing the kitchen. Being proactive gave me a feeling of empowerment, but I felt out of sync with my environment.

Three weeks had passed since my father's death, and I was still painfully aware of his absence, like a face cut out of a photo. And I wasn't used to carrying out the daily activities of my life surrounded by spindly trees and marshmallow skies. I told myself it was a matter of acclimating to a new scene, and accepting that my winterless days were over. So long, sunny SoCal.

Driving my mother to her doctor appointment, I fought my melancholy mood. Cars that had gone unwashed for days whooshed by, their lower halves caked in whitish-brown dirt. *Never in LA*, I thought, longing for my well-kept convertible.

When we arrived at the medical facility, I braced against my mother to keep warm as we hustled toward the nondescript building.

"Don't go so fast," she said. "I can't keep up."

I slowed my pace. "Sorry, but I'm freezing."

My mother wiped her eyes with a tissue, staring at the asphalt like it was a minefield. I put an arm around her, at a loss for words.

Inside the building, we were led through a maze of carpeted hallways by a squat, folder-carrying nurse who kept smiling angelically at my mother and saying things like, "It's so nice to see you," and "You feel good today?" in an accent I couldn't pinpoint, but thought might be Russian. She seemed oblivious to my mother's forlorn state, but maybe I was oversensitive. The nurse dropped her folder in a plastic holder outside an examining room.

"In here, please, my beautiful," she said to my mother.

I went in behind her, put off by the cold, minty-smelling room.

"Sit here," the nurse said to my mother, patting the examining table.

I pulled out the sliding footstool for my mother and she climbed aboard, dangling her legs off the end of the table. I wedged into an aluminum chair, instinctively cataloguing my surroundings: vinyl examining table layered with paper, human anatomy poster, and receptacles filled with Q-tips and cotton balls. It seemed important to pay attention; between my mother and me, I knew I was the only one who would remember this appointment. My mother was ghostlike, in her own world. I wasn't much better off, but I had the advantage of being thirty years younger.

The doctor entered the room and gave my mother a hug. She looked to be in her mid- to late-seventies, though her messily cropped hair projected a youthful athleticism.

I got up and introduced myself, jolted by the realization that I had never chaperoned my mother to a medical appointment. I might not have given it a second thought if it hadn't been for the doctor's tentative response to my extended hand. I felt like a third wheel.

Sliding back to my chair, I focused on my mother.

"I feel so sad," she said to the doctor.

"I know it's hard," said Dr. Post. "But it will get better, in time." Lifting her chin as if on a stage, she said, "Life in mourning is a series of peaks and valleys. You will feel moments of both joy and sorrow."

Her theatrics struck me as odd. Did the doctor offer this bit of wisdom to all her newly widowed patients?

"Let's see what medications you're on," said the doctor, facing her laptop. "I can put you on an antidepressant, but I want to make sure it doesn't conflict with anything you're taking." Tap-tap-tap. "How have you been sleeping?"

"Pretty well," said my mother. "I dream about Peter all the time."

"I wish I did," I said, trying not to sound jealous. My father seemed to have taken a pass on me dream-wise. Did he think I didn't miss him? Was it some sort of test?

"Well, that's good that you dream about your husband," the doctor said. "I know you have a lot of wonderful memories. Let's see… are you still taking the Atorvastatin?"

My mother turned to me with a puzzled look.

"That's the same as Lipitor, right?" I asked.

"Correct," said the doctor, eye-jamming her computer screen. "Yes, she's still taking that."

I remember things visually, and in my mind I could now see the labeling on all of my mother's pill bottles. "Mom takes Actonel first thing in the morning on an empty stomach. Then, after thirty minutes, she takes Lipitor, Lisinopril, and Synthroid. The generic form—Levothyroxine."

The doctor sat up, as if seeing me for the first time. "So, you're the daughter," she said. "Do you live with your mother?"

The daughter? I thought, cringing.

"Not now," I said, "but I will be in the new year."

"Jana's moving here all the way from California," said my mother. "Aren't I lucky?"

"You are," said Dr. Post, unconvincingly, I thought. "I can see you'll have a strong advocate."

Miffed, I realized this was how I would now be defined in the doctor's mind: not as an individual with her own life, but as a proxy for my mother. It was only because I loved my mother so much that I was willing to bite my tongue.

"Why don't we try Zoloft," said Dr. Post. "If that doesn't help, we'll try something else."

At this my mother nodded her head in agreement and said, "That sounds good."

"Zoloft is a time-release medication," the doctor said. "So it won't kick in for about three weeks. And it *may* make you drowsy. Avoid driving if you can, not just because of the medication, but because you're in a bit of a fog right now, and it could be dangerous. But it's important that you get into a routine. What time are you getting up in the morning?"

"Around nine o'clock," said my mother.

"Um… that's not true," I said, distressed. Why had my mother lied?

"Okay," said Dr. Post. "What have you observed?"

I felt like I should be wearing a lab coat. "Yesterday Mom woke up at 1 p.m."

"That's a little late," Dr. Post admitted. "I would like you to get up no later than 9 a.m. Your daughter can help you with that."

I clenched my teeth, thinking *there's that third person language again*. Like I wasn't even in the room. "She can after she moves back," I said.

"Tell you what," said Dr. Post. "Let's see how you do on the Zoloft. I can send the prescription to the drugstore through my computer, or I can print it out for you when we're done here. Which do you prefer?"

"Gee, I don't know," said my mother, glancing at me for the answer.

"Print it out, please," I said. "I'm not sure what drugstore we're going to."

"Okay," said the doctor. "At this point we won't concern ourselves with how late you're sleeping. But I would like you to get out of bed. How is your health otherwise?"

"I have a terrible pain in my back," said my mother, her face creasing into despair.

"Describe the pain to me. Show me exactly where it is."

Tap-tap-tap.

Patient presents with back pain, I imagined her typing. Where was the doctor going with all this? I thought, *my father's dead. Just give her the Zoloft. She'll feel better all over.*

"It's around my waist." My mother reached her hands behind her back. "In this area. It feels like a tight rubber band."

"She had lower back surgery in August," I said, sad all of a sudden. I had visited my parents that month. It was the last time I saw my father alive.

"I would suggest going back to the doctor who did the surgery," Dr. Post said. "Get an x-ray to make sure you've healed properly. You might also want to see a rheumatologist." She stood and faced my mother. "And *I* would like to see you again in a month. I'll print out this Zoloft prescription for you. Be right back."

I felt lightheaded. I hadn't come to the appointment thinking it would sprout a bunch of new ones, creating more work for myself to keep my mother healthy. At the same time, I wanted her to feel better. I decided to start with the x-ray for now, and have Tasha take our mother to the follow-up with Dr. Post in January, when I would be packing up in LA.

The doctor came back into the room and handed me a piece of paper.

"I'll see you both in a month," she said.

"You might see my sister instead of me," I said. Then I realized it probably didn't make a difference to her which one of us showed up. All of us sons and daughters were interchangeable.

AS SOON AS WE GOT HOME, I called to schedule my mother's lower back x-ray as suggested by Dr. Post. There was an opening next week, so I took the appointment. It didn't even occur to me to ask Tasha if she could take our mother in for the x-ray. My sister had used up her bereavement leave and was now back at work, whereas I was in a no man's land of hanging around the house before flying back to California.

After making the appointment, I went into the family room and found my mother by the piano, fixated on a platoon of photographs of her and my father: beaming in front of the lodge they went to every year in Italy; mugging for the camera at their thirty-fifth wedding anniversary; double-dating with my aunt and her beau. Happy smiles everywhere. Wrenching reminders of Dad.

"It's not fair," my mother said, bursting into tears. "He should be here with us."

"Well," I said, "you had fifty-six years together. Sixty, if you count from the day you and Dad first met."

"True," said my mother, "But you always want more."

"Mom, sixty years is a lot more than most people have."

"I know," she said. Her body seemed to collapse within itself. "It's just—we always thought we would grow old together."

"Well… you kind of did, didn't you?"

I thought, *what did they consider old? One hundred? Ninety-five?* Then I realized my mother must have meant growing old in the sense of becoming elderly. I wondered what else I didn't know about their marriage. Who were they when I wasn't around? My emotions spun in all directions. I longed for the cocktail hour to blot out my grief.

A MONTH HAD PASSED since my father's death, and it was almost time for Christmas. But I felt divorced from the holiday.

What worked for the rest of the world seemed to have no bearing on my life. As I drove down the block, I barely noticed the multicolored lights trimming the houses along the way. At the bottom of the street, I stopped and reread my directions to GW Hospital, the site of today's x-ray appointment.

I wound out of the neighborhood, glancing at my mother. Her eyes were closed, head tilted back. I hated seeing her so broken.

"Mom," I said, "have you read any of the book on grief that Trish sent you?"

"I tried to," said my mother, "but it made me feel worse."

"Why...?"

"I don't know, it's just painful," she said, sounding hoarse.

"But it will help put your pain in perspective."

"I suppose you're right," said my mother.

I guided the car to the highway. "I know you weren't keen on writing the remembrance with me, and I understand why, but... maybe it would be good for you to start writing again."

My mother kept quiet.

"Or," I said, "you could go back to the White House." My mother had been a White House volunteer since the first term of the Reagan administration.

"I couldn't," said my mother.

"Mom, you met Michelle Obama. I know you enjoyed that work."

"But I don't feel the same way about it now."

I paused, trying to get a handle on this new version of my mother.

"Did you and Dad ever talk about... well, what you would do if the other died?"

"No," said my mother. "We thought we would live forever."

"Really?"

"We never discussed it," said my mother. "We were having too much fun."

Never discussed it. I couldn't fathom this. The reality of death struck me in my early twenties, when I lost a dear friend to AIDS. I lost another friend to cancer at age twenty-nine.

"Well, Dad *was* getting older," I said. "Maybe I noticed it more because I only saw you guys a few times a year. But when I was here a few months ago, he seemed tired."

"You think so?" said my mother, surprised.

"Yes. I'm not saying he was ready to die, but he seemed physically tired. He worked hard his whole life. It caught up with him."

"But he left so quickly," said my mother, her head falling back.

"I know. But it's not like he planned it that way. And you had a lot of amazing years together."

"That makes it worse," she said, opening her purse, pulling out a tissue.

I let out a long breath, thinking *I give up.*

WHEN WE ARRIVED at the hospital, I escorted my mother up the elevator and into a waiting area, which seemed more like a holding pen with its packed-in rows of chairs. To the left of a wall-mounted television was a door that heaved open and closed, like the entrance to Oz. I checked my mother in, tired of clinical settings, barely able to recall my days as a woman beholden to no one.

A few minutes later, I followed my mother into an examining room not much bigger than the handicap stall in a restroom. As we awaited the arrival of Dr. Shin, the surgeon who had performed my mother's lower back surgery, I absorbed my surroundings: a numbing déjà vu blend of beige and white, cotton and gauze, and a vinyl examining table fitted with disposable paper.

All of a sudden the air was punctured with short gasping sounds.

"Why did he have to die?" my mother said, weeping. "He was so handsome. So tall."

Again? I thought, flustered. I found a tissue and handed it to her.

"Oh, Jana," said my mother, wiping her eyes. "What am I going to do?"

"Keep living," I said, putting an arm around her as I had so many times before. I felt like I was on a repeater reel. "That's all you can do. I think that's what Dad would want."

"Thank God he doesn't have to see me like this," said my mother.

"Maybe he *can* see you," I said. "Apparently he's still wandering the earth, on his forty-day journey. For all we know he could be right here in this room. If he is, he's probably bummed to see you so sad. He probably wants you to start living again."

My mother contemplated this, gazing at the floor. Just then Dr. Shin entered the room—my rescuer. I felt drained from my spontaneous pep talk. I introduced myself, watching as the doctor looked apprehensively at my teary-eyed mother.

"My father died recently," I said, to spare him any further confusion.

"I'm sorry," said Dr. Shin, moving farther into the room.

"He went so quickly," said my mother, bypassing *hello* entirely.

"So…" the doctor said, regrouping, "we did your surgery about four months ago. How is your back feeling now?"

"Not bad," said my mother.

I was shocked. "But Mom, last week you said it was killing you."

"Well, it comes and goes," said my mother.

"If that's the case," said the doctor, "physical therapy might be in order. But let's get an x-ray first, and see how you're healing." He told my mother to take off everything but her stockings and bra, and put on a gown. Then he left the room.

"Would you undo me?" said my mother.

I unzipped her dress, then helped her get into her hospital gown, partly to speed things along, but also because my mother seemed so frail, nothing at all like the energetic Mom I'd grown up with, the one who had a hard time sitting still. After the x-ray was taken, I helped her back into her dress, and then sank into a chair against the wall.

"Thank you," said my mother. She sat next to me and slipped into her Ferragamos, wriggling her stocking feet into the shoes. Then she tilted her head back and closed her eyes.

Gone again, I thought, feeling anxious. The book on grief didn't seem to be doing my mother any good. I had to try something else.

"Mom," I said, "how would you feel about getting some grief counseling?"

She hesitated. "I don't think so."

I pretended not to hear her. "The county has a service where grief counselors make home visits. I think it would be good for you to talk with someone."

"I talk with you," said my mother.

"It's not the same," I said, mortified at the thought of my pep talks being open-ended. "For one thing I'm not a trained counselor. And I've got my own feelings of grief to process, and a new life to create, which will be hard enough without having to worry about how sad you are."

"You don't have to worry about me," said my mother.

"I don't have to, but I will because I love you. Please give the counseling some thought."

"Okay," she said. "I'll think about it."

I felt hopeful. It wasn't a yes, but it wasn't a no, either.

When Dr. Shin finally came back into the room, he explained that the x-rays showed the L4 and L5 (or was it L3 and L4?) discs in my mother's spinal cord had fused perfectly after her surgery. He recommended physical therapy to keep her pain in check, and then said something about a nerve-stimulating device called a T.E.N.S. unit.

"Medicare will pay for it," he said, "but there's a specific way to fill out the form. Excuse me." The doctor poked his head out the door, then came back into the room, handing me a business card. "Call this number. They'll tell you exactly how to place the order. And I'll give you a prescription for Lidoderm."

He started writing on a pad. "It's a medicated patch, for the pain area. You can also try Extra Strength Tylenol. Sometimes that's more effective than anything."

He tore off the prescription and held it out for my immobile mother.

I intercepted the paper, lips parted in a stupor, the circuitry in my brain overloaded. I didn't know where to begin. The patches? The T.E.N.S. unit? Physical therapy? The doctor told my mother to come back in three months. He wished her well and left the room.

"We'll have to deal with all this when I get back from LA," I said.

"That's fine," said my mother. "I'll be okay."

I wasn't convinced, but I helped her into her coat anyway, and we exited the examining room, pushing through the big, white door in the direction of the holding pen.

TEARS FELL, AGAIN AND AGAIN. Christmas and the new year came and went in a haze of toasts to my father and muddling through the holidays made wretched by his absence. I was relieved when Zoë came up from Florida to share the emotional load. It also helped when Tasha came by on the weekends. With my sisters in the house, the bleak atmosphere seemed to dissipate, and I felt happier knowing I wasn't the only fully functioning person around.

When I told Tasha about our mother's need for a follow-up appointment with Dr. Post, she waved a hand and said, "I'll take her. No problem." Like she was tossing around a football.

Agitated, I said, "Did you revisit the idea of grief counseling with Mom?" I had asked her to bring it up so I wasn't the only one promoting the idea.

"I did," said Tasha. "Mom said, 'I grieve in my own way.'" Meaning *without help from outsiders.* "Maybe she'll feel differently in a few weeks," Tasha added.

In my mind, *a few weeks* of my mother being so out of it felt more like a year. I thought she needed counseling *now.* "Maybe if we offer to go with her," I said, "she'll change her mind."

"Maybe," said my sister. She turned sober, adding, "We're going to get through this."

I guess her words were meant to reassure me, but they rang hollow in my ears. I had never seen my mother so weepy and removed from everyday life. Her grief was starting to depress me. I kept telling myself that I just needed to get away from it for a while, and get my life back on track. I was tired of living out of a suitcase. I needed to return to LA and close out that chapter of my life.

Clinging to the positive, I took comfort in the praises for my father's remembrance, published in the *Herald* at the end of the year. Friends and relatives sent flattering e-mails, and when I showed the article to my mother, she read it with tears of joy.

"You did a beautiful job," she said.

"They printed it almost exactly as I wrote it," I said, amazed.

"What a guy," said my mother, shaking her head at the photo of my father.

It was prominent on the page, in the second of four columns of copy. In the photo my father was glancing off camera, with his mouth ajar, in an expectant smile. His hazel eyes were lit up like a switchboard, as if he were processing several thoughts at once. My father looked happy.

It had only been forty days since my father's death, but it seemed like much longer, maybe because going through two holidays without him right away felt like a never-ending test of endurance. Between his death, my mother's unraveling, and the process of deciding my next steps, I felt like I'd experienced the full spectrum of emotions, forty different ways.

But standing next to my mother now, in the front row of the church, I felt an inner peace. Gone was the heartache of my previous visit to St. George's, when I kissed my father goodbye in his casket. On this Sunday of his forty-day memorial service, I dared to feel hopeful about my unwritten future. I scanned the church, warmed by the multigenerational faces around me, and swatches of bright-colored clothes. The last time I was here, the pews were awash in black.

I faced the priest on the altar. He was giving the Divine Liturgy, flanked on either side by three interlocking screens, trimmed in gold and rounded at the top, with Byzantine religious figures on each set against brilliant teal tiles. The only figures I recognized were Christ on the priest's right, and the Virgin Mary on the left. I studied the six panels, intrigued by the images. After the hazy experience of my father's funeral, I felt like I was seeing the church anew. A large, gold cross was mounted on the back wall, with rays of white light radiating from the cross. Above this was a towering depiction of the Virgin Mary in a glimmering, coral-and-gold robe, set against sea blue tiles.

The scenery was enchanting, but I couldn't see myself coming back for more. I was too much of a Doubting Thomas.

"Did you see this?" I said to my mother, pointing to a small notice in the program announcing today's prayer *for the repose of the departed, Peter E. Panarites.*

My mother took the program, nodding sadly as she read it, then returned the paper to me.

A cloth-covered cart was wheeled to the front of the altar, over the white marble floor. On top of the cart was a lit candle and a white loaf known as the *kollyva*, a ritual offering on behalf of the deceased. The priest began chanting in Greek and English, reading from the Bible, swinging the chain of bells before the *kollyva*. Smoke filled the air, along with the pungent aroma of incense. I closed my eyes, thinking about my father, remembering our last hug, curbside at Dulles airport, on my last visit east. "Call us when you get to LA," I heard him saying. "Love you, dear." I opened my eyes to keep from crying, though they were already wet.

"Dear Lord," said the priest, "we ask that you restore your dearly departed servant, Peter Panarites, to the divine image in which he was created, and ask you to forgive his sins and give rest to his soul."

As the priest continued reading, I looked at the *kollyva* and felt a fleeting sadness for my father's final leaving. The shape of the loaf was symbolic: an oval mound, suggestive of a burial grave. I reminded myself that the seeds in the loaf symbolized the life-giving aspect of death and eternal life in resurrection. I didn't believe in the afterlife, but I knew my father's genes had been passed on to me, and that he would remain alive in my heart. That was his *life after death* for me.

The priest did his *stavro*, set down the Bible, and circled the *kollyva*, swinging the chain of bells in front of it as he sang the refrain: "E – o – ni – a i mni – mi... E – o – ni – a i mni – mi... E – o – ni – a af – ton i mni – mi." *May his memory be eternal.* The refrain echoed through the church as parishioners joined in the chanting. A few moments later the priest made a motion for everyone to sit down. I wiped my eyes, turning to my mother.

"I'm glad that's over," I said, relieved more than comforted. I appreciated the prayers, but I was eager to unburden myself from the heaviness of death. I wanted to embrace the beauty of life.

DURING THE COFFEE HOUR in the gym located next to the chapel, I nibbled on a piece of *kollyva*, feeling out of place yet also at home. I couldn't recall the last time I had set foot in the gym, or if I had ever set foot in it at all. It was possible I had played basketball here during my years on the Greek youth team. Then again it was also possible that this wing was built later, long after I moved away. I felt like I should know some of the churchgoers, but they looked a lot younger than me.

"I don't recognize any of these people," I said to Tasha's friend, the one she had wanted to introduce me to. What did she say her name was?

"That's no surprise," said the gal with the winning smile. "The congregation has probably quadrupled in size since your family started coming here."

Looks-wise she reminded me of Elizabeth Taylor. I guessed she was in her early fifties. Whatever her age (or name), I could tell we would get along because she seemed out of place like me. She was sizing up the crowd with a mix of amusement and curiosity, as if studying a rare species.

"How's your mother doing?" she said under her breath, because my mother was standing nearby, miraculously engaged in conversation, punctuated by nervous sips of coffee.

"It's day to day," I said.

"It must be so hard for her." She paused. "How are *you* doing?"

"Oh—I guess I'm all right. Thanks for asking."

I hadn't seen that one coming. Usually everyone asked about my mother, but now I realized that answering questions on her behalf obscured my own feelings of grief. It didn't help that after a lifetime of ricocheting from one job to the next, I was conditioned to thinking positive just to survive.

"Tasha always talks about 'the sister who lives in California,'" said my new friend, making air quotes. "And now we finally meet!"

"Yes. She tells me you're a great cook." I felt silly pulling the topic out of thin air, but it was one of the few things Tasha had told me about her that I could remember.

"Oh, no," she said, laughing. "My *mother* is a great cook. She's up there in the pantheon, like a Greek goddess. No matter how hard I try, I will never reach her status."

"So, you're sort of on the D-List?" I asked, smiling. I liked her self-deprecating humor.

"Exactly! That's me. My life on the Greek D-List."

"I have an idea," I said, thinking *maybe we can work together*. "But I don't want to talk about it yet. Let's have lunch when I get back from LA."

"Sounds great."

And there I was, mapping out my future. My father's forty-day journey had come to an end; tomorrow I would begin my journey back to California, to pack up and drive back east. Back to the beginning.

2
Hollywood Ending

Forty-one days since Dad's death.

"Please go back inside," I said. "You're going to catch a cold."

My mother was standing under the raised door of the garage, staving off the winter air in her fluffy, lavender bathrobe. Her hair was disheveled, her eyes sleepy and shrunken in their sockets. She looked like a crestfallen Yoda.

It was the morning of my departure for LA. Saying goodbye to my mother felt ominous, as if the moment I looked away from her something awful might happen. She might fall and break a hip because she wasn't paying attention, or accidentally set off a fire in the kitchen. More than once now, she had left the oven on, despite my *Turn Oven Off* sign taped to the wall.

"I'm waiting until the cab leaves," said my mother.

"It's freezing out here," I said.

"I don't care."

Her stubbornness was testing my nerves. "Well, I do," I said. "I don't want you getting sick on my account."

"I got it," said the driver, blowing into his hands as he got out of the taxi. He took the luggage out of my hands, dropped it in the trunk, slammed it shut, and hurried inside the cab.

"Tasha will be coming by after work," I said to my mother, "and she'll stay with you all week so you won't be alone. Then Thea will take over."

My mother nodded bravely, but her eyes were wet.

"I'll be back in three weeks," I said, hugging her, knowing it wouldn't be soon enough. "Now please—go inside."

"I will in a minute," she said.

I climbed into the cab and shut the door, unnerved by her defiance. As the car rolled off the driveway, I waved through the window. My mother raised an arm, and then turned to go inside. I hoped she remembered to lock the basement door.

IT WAS MID AFTERNOON by the time the plane landed at LAX. I corralled my luggage and made my way out of the terminal, overtaken by the acrid smell of exhaust fumes. Beyond the concrete pillars was a brilliant sheet of sunlight. I couldn't wait to feel its warmth. I climbed into a yellow cab, and gave the driver my address in West Hollywood. As we exited the airport, I opened my window, comforted by the warm breeze and view of palm trees. I found my BlackBerry and speed-dialed my mother. By now, checking in at all travel points was mandatory.

"Hi Mom." The line was quiet. "Hello?"

"Yes, I—sorry… I dropped the phone. So you made it safely."

"I did," I said.

"And when will you be back?"

"Three weeks," I said, her neediness making me jumpy. I glanced at my watch. It was 6:30 p.m. on the East Coast. "What did you do today?"

"Slept, mostly," said my mother.

"Oh, Mom." I let out a sigh. "Well, Tasha should be there soon, to have dinner with you."

"Okay. I have to go now," said my mother. "I love you."

I heard an abrupt click, and flipped the phone around in front of me as if waiting for it to speak. "Love you, too."

THE TAXI TURNED UP North Sycamore Avenue. I felt wistful, certain I would miss the stylish, art deco buildings lining the street, and gargantuan palm trees engulfing each entrance. I would also miss days like today when it was seventy-five degrees in January.

"It's coming up on the right," I said. "See the yellow Volkswagen?"

The driver didn't say anything, but I guess he got my meaning because a few moments later we were parked at an angle behind the Bug, near my two-story stucco building. I got out and stared at the cracked driveway my neighbor Greg had scurried up six weeks ago to deliver the unthinkable news that my father was dead. I felt like a different person now, less patient, moving through life with the tunnel vision of a Secret Service agent. I paid the driver, gathered my luggage, and rolled it up the driveway. I entered the back door of the building, and opened the door into my apartment.

The air in the kitchen was cool and close. I felt hemmed in. I opened one of the windows above the sink, remembering the horrifying image of Greg's fingers rapping on the window on the morning of my father's death. Unsteady, I leaned against the sink. I gathered myself together and then slowly moved into the living room. I stared at the parquet wood flooring, white stucco walls, and stylish arches on either side of the storage closet. I felt alienated from my surroundings, as if they were part of a long forgotten past. *Focus*, I thought. *Get to the task at hand.*

I powered up my laptop and opened one of the casement windows to let in some fresh air. A breeze came in and I felt calmer, until I sat at the desk and surveyed the apartment. In the next three weeks I had to get rid of a couch, a three-drawer dresser, bookcases, dining table, chairs, a queen-size bed, area rugs, floor lamps, table lamps, pots, pans, placemats, and all manner of bric-a-brac. *Holy shit*, I thought. *What if I can't sell everything?*

I logged onto Craigslist. The best way to get rid of everything was to list it at rock bottom prices. In the worst-case scenario, a junk removal company could be hired to cart off unsold items. But how would that unfold? How much lead-time would the company need? Selling everything was the best option. I needed to see things go out the door, to see with my own eyes that this chapter of my life was ending. I also needed the cash, for tolls on the drive east, and pit stops for gas and food.

I began writing up the Craigslist ad, taking furniture measurements, noting dimensions, and creating an inventory.

An hour later, my possessions were listed on the Internet for all comers. I zeroed in on the suitcase I had yet to unpack from my flight. The sound of my BlackBerry ringing cut through the quiet of the apartment. I answered the phone, unfamiliar with the number on the screen.

"Hello?"

"Hi. I'm calling about the mattress and box spring. Are they still available?"

"Uh… yes," I said, thinking *still available? I just put up the ad!*

"Cool. Can I get it tonight?"

"Sure," I said. "What time?"

"How's eight-thirty?"

"I'll be here." I gave the caller the address and hung up, thinking it was a good thing I'd bought an inflatable mattress. I would be sleeping on it tonight, and for the next three weeks.

THE NEXT DAY I BEGAN the marathon process of boxing up clothes, artwork, electronics, and a few dozen books, pushing five large containers into a corner for shipping east. The hours passed quickly from one sunny day to the next. I barely noticed the beautiful weather—which I'd become accustomed to in Southern California—too preoccupied with making bulk donations to Out of the Closet thrift store, and tending to the parade of strangers in my apartment, buying things I'd posted on Craigslist. I worked feverishly, worried I wouldn't finish in time, but then one day, I completely lost my momentum.

My undoing was a family photograph, taken nine months ago at USC. Mom, Dad, my sisters and brother-in-law had all flown out for my master's degree graduation ceremony, and there they were on campus, on a golden California day. Staring at the photo, I slid to the hardwood floor, transfixed by the image, tears in my eyes. Was that me in the middle of the photo, beaming in cap and gown? That person seemed younger and more laid back than the person I was now: a baby boomer on a mission, on intimate terms with death. And there was my mother in the photo, smiling coolly, stylish as always in her magenta linen slacks and seashell Nehru jacket. She, too, appeared different: invincible, nothing like the heartbroken mother I said goodbye to when I left DC. Next to her in the photo was my dapper, jovial father. I had seen him on one more occasion since the time of this photo: when I flew to DC just before Labor Day for a visit with my parents. At the end of the visit, my father had driven me to Dulles airport, and set my bulging duffel bag on the ground in front of the US Airways terminal before kissing me goodbye. Had the act of lifting the bag strained his heart? Should I have lifted the bag myself? Our curbside hug was the last we would ever have.

Lowering the photo, I looked at my apartment, emptied of its furnishings, stunned at how quickly my life had changed. Just as the apartment had been dismantled, so, too, had I. But I was in the process of being reassembled, too. I had found it hard to grieve for my father, and now I knew why: before I could grieve for him, I needed to grieve for my life on the West Coast, lived on two separate occasions, twenty years apart. I wasn't quite done with LA after all.

If I harbored any doubts about leaving California, the last week put them to rest when it rained for six days straight.

Holed up in my echo chamber of an apartment, drained of furniture, I stared at the gushing grey skies thinking, *I'm living in Seattle.*

In an attempt to escape my solitary confinement, I called every friend I had left in LA: "Are you free for drinks?" When I called my mother to check up on her (and while away the hours), she seemed as sleepy as when I left her.

"What time is it?" my mother said.

"Two p.m. your time," I said, hearing her yawn.

"Gosh, is it that late?" said my mother.

"Yes," I said, tensing up at her lethargic state. "Are you still in your pajamas?"

"Yes," she admitted.

"Oh, Mom…."

"Could you tell me how to use the coffee maker?" she said.

"Sure." I threw in the towel, thinking *she doesn't know how to use the coffee maker?* I tutored my mother on the phone, giving her step-by-step instructions.

Finally, it stopped raining on the day before I left LA, so I drove up to Malibu for one last look at the ocean. It was overcast at the beach, and no one was around except the hard-core surfers. I parked on a thin shoulder of the road, and lowered myself down a grassy cliff side to the pebble-stained shore.

The air felt damp and cooler than farther inland. The tide was out, and tiny waves were curling up on the shore. I scanned the breadth of the cove, stretched out along the coast. To my right was a pack of surfers, paddling through tranquil, unpromising waters. I slid off my flip-flops and moved in their direction, soothed by the cold, wet sand pressing against the undersides of my feet.

I perched on a wood pillar facing the ocean, wrapping my arms around my waist as I eyed the infinite horizon. The sky was whitish black, like charcoal smudged on parchment. In the distance a ribbon of sunlight framed the clouds. I held my gaze on the strip of light, and then lowered my head, sweeping my toes back and forth in the sand. If only I knew how my future would play out. I longed for certainty. But I knew that, like so much of Hollywood, certainty was an illusion.

THE NEXT MORNING I sprang out of bed at 8 a.m. Whatever feelings of anxiety I'd gone to bed with were washed away by daylight, replaced by excitement for the road trip ahead. I had already tanked up and loaded most of my possessions into the car. The only thing left to do was roll up and pack the Aerobed.

I uncorked the inflatable bed and flopped on the billowy plastic until it pancaked to the floor. I rolled it up, dragged it outside, and heaved the bag into the back seat of my car. Opening the trunk, I tucked a bottle of Veuve Clicquot champagne into the left corner. Friends from San Francisco had given it to me after graduating from USC, but I hadn't opened it that day, nor had I found the right occasion afterward. I shut the trunk and gazed at the building I had lived in for the past seven years, the sun cascading brightly on the stucco walls. Standing there in silence, I felt totally alone, the way you feel in LA when the weather is perfect, but there's no one around to share it with.

Empty LA. I got in the car and strapped on my seatbelt. Reaching for my BlackBerry, I speed-dialed my mother. It was 11:30 a.m. on the East Coast.

"Heh… hello," she said groggily, picking up.

"Hi Mom, it's me," I said, guessing she was still in bed, tamping down my frustration. "I just wanted to let you know I'm leaving."

"Be careful on the road," she said.

"I will."

"And don't talk to strangers."

"Cute," I said, thinking *that's the old Mom*. "Get out of bed and get on your exercise bike."

"Okay, dear," she moaned.

"I'll call you when I get to Tucson. Bye for now."

"Bye, dear," said my mother.

I hung up, shifted into drive, and headed for the 10 east freeway. It was a Sunday, the only day of the week when the tangle of freeways surrounding LA wasn't congested.

The farther east I drove, the more relaxed my body felt. But the 10 east was a road I had traveled many times, crawling in traffic to get to the beach or visit friends in Palm Springs, so at first the trip didn't seem to involve a finality. To feel in my bones that I was leaving the West Coast for good, I had to get beyond familiar territory and enter the unknown, to see and feel something at ground level that I hadn't experienced during my time in LA.

The wide-open landscape of western Arizona was where I felt a physical separation between my past and the future. I gaped in awe at the flat landscape on either side of the road. It produced an optical illusion, shrinking the space between earth and sky. In the distance were magnificent, white-specked mountains, like an otherworld Lost Horizon. The view was humbling and inspiring; it offered the possibility of something new, the fresh start I craved and was now moving toward.

I had planned to call one or two friends from the road, but as I whizzed forward, I realized the urge to speak had left my mind. There were no words to convey my emotions, and I didn't want to share them anyway. They were too overwhelming.

You're actually doing it, I thought. *You're starting your life over at age fifty.*

A flash of fear cut through my brain, but the feeling quickly switched to euphoria, the act of moving forward invigorating. I told myself to hold onto that feeling and focus on the positive: I was remaking my life in a place that had a lower than average unemployment rate. I was also helping my mother in her time of need. Of course, there would be challenges, but I would get through them as I always had. I had gotten through my father's death. What could be worse than that? *My father's death.* I repeated the words aloud, to get used to the fact that he wasn't coming back.

My mind drifted endlessly with each passing hour. I thought about where I might live after my time in Maryland. Because in my mind this was definitely a one-year deal. Could I live in New York again? No. Sixteen years was enough. Chicago? Freezing rain came to mind, along with four-foot banks of snow. No thanks. Not after sunny SoCal. San Francisco? No. California was off the table. Too far from family. I wanted to be near my family. Now more than ever, I needed their love and strength. So why was I already thinking about leaving them? *Austin,* I thought, my mind going off in every direction. I'd heard it had a vibrant arts scene. But Austin was in Texas, the death penalty capital of the nation. Austin was a reach. Why not spend part of the year in Europe? I had never been to Italy, but my cousin DeAnna was on the verge of moving to Tuscany. Maybe I could rent a villa there for six months of the year.

So many possibilities offered up on the road: the neutral ground, neither here nor there. I felt safe in that space of no commitment, where the future was no further ahead than the strip of asphalt beyond my car.

The entire journey east, I felt my father was guiding me home. He seemed to be protecting me, as if even in death he couldn't refrain from doing his job as a parent. That had to be why in the worst days of winter I encountered clear skies from coast to coast, and managed to stay ahead of all the bad weather. I didn't notice this phenomenon at first, intent on tackling the trip one leg at a time: waking up, checking out of my hotel room, and hitting the road by 7:00 a.m.

And so it was that I arrived in Midland, Texas, on a bright, clear day. I checked into the Hilton, exhausted. I called my mother, ate dinner, watched the news, and went to bed. The next morning, after I left Midland, rain soaked the city. Ten hours later I arrived in sunny Little Rock, Arkansas, checked into my hotel, and repeated my routine. The next morning, I set off for Nashville under a radiant sky. Later, back in Little Rock, the city was deluged with rain and snow. I left Nashville on a sunlit morning, and encountered blue skies all through the lush countryside before arriving in North Bethesda. The next day in Nashville it snowed. At every step of the way, I had escaped inclement weather.

"You have no idea how lucky you were," my brother-in-law said.

Was it luck? Or was it my father keeping me safe on the road? I didn't have the answer. The only thing I knew was, in my experience, a run of luck was always followed by a wave of misfortune.

3

The Landing

Two months since Dad's death.

I COULD BARELY REMEMBER leaving LA, but I believed today was Thursday. The car's glowing dashboard lights told me it was 8:30 p.m. My rear end felt numb, as if it had melded with the beaded seat cover, and my eyes felt like tiny knots, hardened from overconcentration. Finally, at the top of the cul-de-sac, I set eyes on our family home.

The walkway lights were on as usual in anticipation of an evening visitor. *No turning back now*, I thought, tensing up. *This is your last stop.* I pulled into the driveway, shut off the engine, and removed the bottle of champagne from my travel cooler. Cold air engulfed me as I cracked open the car door. I scurried up the lawn and clacked the front door knocker impatiently, thinking, *come on Mom*. I bounced up and down to stay warm. At last my mother opened the door. She stepped back like a spooked cat.

"Come in, dear, and close the door," she said, "It's cold out."

"You got that right." I fell into her arms, feeling like a child again in the warmth of her parental embrace. "I made it." I held onto her, gathering my emotions.

"You poor dear," said my mother. "You must be exhausted."

"I am. I've been on the road for twelve hours."

"Oh, Jana—you shouldn't have pushed yourself like that."

In the mirror I saw my face, ashen as a ghoul in *Night of the Living Dead*. My eyes were bloodshot, hair matted as if I'd been sleeping on it for days. I turned away, frightened by my reflection.

"We should open this," I said, holding up the champagne.

My mother's eyes came alive just briefly. "I'll get some glasses," she said, inching toward the formal dining room.

I fell in behind her, disoriented, hyper aware of my father's absence. All of a sudden the homecoming hit me like a blast of hot air. *This is it.* I trembled. *From now on it's just Mom and me.* I was here to stay—to start over in my new home. My old home *and* my new home. With my grief-stricken, elderly mother. The walls seemed to be closing in on me. I told myself to breathe, that I felt claustrophobic because the house was so dark inside.

Inside the kitchen, I fumbled for a dimmer switch and brought up the recessed lights. I felt better. But I was taken aback by the newspapers scattered across the breakfast table and mail stacked on the counter, littered with crumbs and dirty dishes. How could my mother live with this mess? This wasn't like her at all. Or was it?

Thrown off by the disarray, I swayed past the fridge, automatically checking the oven and stove to make sure nothing was on (all clear). I sat at the breakfast table and cleared away the newspapers, unearthing a patch of marble. Setting the champagne on the table, I unpeeled the foil.

"Did Tasha come by today?" I said.

My mother came into the kitchen, pensive, fluted glasses in hand.

Why couldn't she answer such a simple question without stopping to think about it?

"Yes," my mother said at last. "We had an early dinner, and she left after that. Why don't you call and tell her you're here?"

"I'm too tired," I said. "You know I'm here, and that's all that matters."

I popped the champagne cork and filled both glasses, clinking with my mother.

"Cheers," I said. "To the next chapter. For both of us."

My mood lifted with a sip of the icy champagne. I tried imagining what the *next chapter* looked like, but it was still fuzzy on so many levels: work, social life, a world without Dad, my mother as a widow. Blank pages all, waiting to be filled in.

"Some boxes came for you," said my mother. "They're in the garage."

"Wow, that was fast. Are any of them damaged?"

"I don't think so. What's in them?"

"Nothing much," I said. "Just the entire contents of my life. Besides what's in my car."

I wasn't sure what unsettled me more: the reality of my response, or the fact that it didn't seem to occur to my mother that the boxes were filled with my belongings. What else would they contain?

"I'm going upstairs," said my mother, sliding her glass to the center of the table. She gave me a tender, completely exposed look. I felt a sudden protectiveness toward her. "I'm so glad you're here," she added.

"Me too." I gave her a hug, then watched as she left the room.

The mess on the kitchen counter caught my eye. My mother had drifted right past it without giving it a second thought, as if the pile could grow and expand, and she would just let it all slide. That reminded me: I had to call the housekeeper recommended by one of my cousins, when I was home for the funeral. I needed to get us on a bimonthly cleaning schedule. *And I should get one of those dry eraser boards*, I thought, falling into production coordinator mode. A wall calendar, to keep track of appointments, and to prod Mom into putting some structure in her life. She couldn't just sleep all day, as she had been doing for the past weeks.

I took another sip of my champagne, tired but too wired to go to bed. I looked at the photographs on the shelf: Mom and Dad chatting at a posh DC dinner; my mother in various poses from her White House volunteer days—a Rose Garden handshake with Nancy Reagan, a towering Bill Clinton putting his paw on my mother's shoulder, her eyes shining brightly. I couldn't remember the last time I'd seen her smile in such a relaxed, unguarded way. I wanted to see my mother smile like that again. I wanted to make us both laugh. I was tired of the choking grip of death that permeated our house.

Determinedly, I gulped my champagne. I stared at the red-and-white-flecked marble table before me, thinking about all the family meals taken there and our endless bantering. We were all interrupters, my father being somewhat the exception, no doubt realizing that surrounded by four opinionated women, it was pointless to try and hold the floor. But those meals were so long ago. More recently it was just Mom, Dad, and me on visits east. And now it was just Mom and me. I couldn't quite grasp where I was. I knew I had been raised in this house, but having been gone for nearly thirty years, I felt like a visitor.

I finished my champagne and went to turn off the light in the alcove. Beneath the wall-mounted phone, I saw a cache of notes. I picked them up, feeling faint at the sight of my father's penciled handwriting. The top note read: "Buongiorno, Eleni mou, I make-a dee coffee for you, to start the machine my dear, just press-a dee button here." *Eleni mou* translated in Greek as *my Helen*. An arrow on the note pointed in the direction of the button. The next note contained nothing more than the word "Tsa!"—a Greek exclamation of surprise. I put the notes back, unable to read any more.

I shut off the light, tidied up the kitchen, and headed upstairs. At the top floor landing I hesitated, clasping at the railing. The door to my father's bathroom was closed, the same as it had been before I left for California. Stealthily I entered, and stood at the marble sink. I opened the mirrored cabinet, jarred by the shaving brush on the inner ledge, the silver Gillette razor, and red-striped can of Barbasol. I removed the black comb from the lower ledge, stared at it, and put it back. Exhaling, I closed the cabinet and studied the white tile floor, imagining my father lying there on the brink of death. I looked around, confused. How could an event of such magnitude occur in such a drab, utilitarian space?

Something didn't add up. The way my father died was like a myth that made no sense. I needed to revisit what I'd been told and possibly revise the story. What piece of wood or marble had caused the cut on my father's temple? Had he fallen forward, against the sink? Or to the right, on the window ledge? Which direction was he facing when my mother found him on the floor?

Bending at the knees, I examined a scarlet pinprick in the grout, flinching at the sight of the hardened drop of blood. Based on its location and the patched-over cut above my father's eye that I'd seen at the wake, I decided that he had collapsed onto the right side of his body. This meant he was facing the toilet when my mother found him. The base of the toilet was the last thing my father saw, unless he'd gotten a glimpse of my mother as she begged him not to leave her. It seemed possible that my father was still conscious then, and that the last thing he saw was my mother's face. Their eyes could have met one last time.

I exited the bathroom believing this was how my father left us. That was my myth.

4

The Road of Trials

Two-and-a-half months since Dad's death.

Once I unpacked the boxes from California, I felt less like a visitor and more like a long-term tenant, if not a bonafide resident. My airy surroundings were liberating after being confined to apartments for thirty years. But I was troubled by the shapelessness of my mother's life. She spent her hours taking naps or glued to the television. But I had my own life to rebuild, so I pressed on with that goal. For the first few days I was so busy unpacking, buying groceries, and laying in a supply of firewood that I felt like a blip on my mother's radar.

Falling back in time and spinning forward into the future, I lugged the wicker furniture from my old bedroom down to the basement for Goodwill pick-up, and replaced it with my father's tall, mahogany dresser, first removing the drawers to make it easier to carry. I halted, seeing my father's sweaters in the bottom drawer. I removed a brown, V-neck cashmere, pressed the soft fabric against my face, and then tried it on. The sleeves fell beyond my fingers, but the sweater was cozy and it was Dad's. I would keep it. In the dresser's top drawer I discovered my father's cufflinks, a pair of opera glasses, and several watches. I tried on the Wenger Swiss Army watch, securing the worn leather strap around my wrist. *That looks pretty good*, I thought. But then my eyes filled with tears, and I started gasping. I took off the watch and put it back in the dresser, stopping at a cluster of white plastic strips, two-inches long. What were these? I picked one up, realizing I used these same strips with my fitted, Banana Republic dress shirts. They went in at the back of the collar, on the ends. Smiling sadly, I put the strip back in the drawer and emptied the others.

    I transformed the rest of my old bedroom with books and photos brought from LA, and the echoes of my childhood receded into the walls. It was still strange to be there, as if I were living in a bed and breakfast I returned to year after year, but the sanctuary would serve me well.

From tracking it online I saw that my cherished Danish Modern writing desk, shipped from California, was ready for pick-up at a warehouse in Hagerstown. The desk wouldn't fit in my sports car, but it would probably fit in the trunk of my mother's old Mercedes. I went looking for her to let her know I would be using her car for a few hours.

    I found my mother in the family room, laying face up on the couch, with her eyes closed. Seeing her out flat like that,

I instinctively flipped into death mode, and imagined her in a coffin. *Dammit*, I thought, looking away. *Why can't I get those thoughts out of my head?*

"Stay in the present," I said, in a low voice.

"Were you talking to me?"

"Oh… hi. I thought you were sleeping."

"I'm sort of drifting in and out," she said. "What are you up to?"

"I'm going to Hagerstown to pick up my writing desk."

"I'll come with you," she said, stripping off her blanket. "I don't want you going up there alone." As if Hagerstown had been taken over by the Taliban.

"Um… okay." I was hoping to have some time to myself, but maybe now would be a good time to bring up the topic of grief counseling again. In the car, once we got underway.

Downstairs in the garage, I hit the automatic door opener and the panel rolled up behind my mother's car. It was fully raised by the time she appeared in the doorway.

"My car or yours?" said my mother.

I stopped. "Yours." Hadn't she noticed the door behind her car was up? The one behind mine was closed. I locked up the house, downplaying my mother's foggy state of mind. Maybe her medications needed tweaking. I climbed into the car and started the engine.

"Buckle up, please," I said, backing out of the garage.

My mother fished for her seatbelt like it was a new invention, and in a moment I heard a click. As we tailed off the driveway, I saw her eying my father's Jaguar parked at the curb.

"When are we going to sell that?" she said, whimpering.

"Soon."

"It's so painful to look at."

"I know."

I reached over and clasped one of her hands, wishing I could erase her sorrow even as I battled my own. My mother closed her eyes and tilted her seat back. She was heading off to dreamland. I remembered her ability to "flake out" as she called it, under any circumstance. My mother could sleep through turbulence, train delays, you name it. But here in the car I knew she was flaking out to dream about my deceased father, because that was her way of being "with him." But when she was "with him" I felt deserted, as if my company wasn't good enough for her. My mother didn't want me *going up there alone* to Hagerstown, but I might as well have been alone, with her sleeping the whole way. Frustrated, I told myself I was being selfish, that no matter how much I missed my father it was much worse for her. But I had to push the grief counseling, or these silences might never end. I had to catch my mother off guard, like I did this morning when she replayed her latest dream.

"What was this one about?" I said.

"Your Dad and I were having a wonderful time at a party," said my mother. "But then at the end of the night, when I put out my hand, he wouldn't take it."

"Why?" It was impossible to imagine my father rejecting her in any way.

"He said I couldn't go with him because I still had work to do on earth."

"Huh. What sort of work do you think he was referring to?" I asked, trying to steer the conversation to the next phase of her life.

My mother was about to take a sip of her orange juice, but then stopped, surprised. She pondered my question for a fraction of a second.

"Who knows," she said, downing her glass of OJ.

Her apathy floored me. But I took a message from the dream: my father's refusal to take her hand meant I should be equally firm with my mother.

"Mom," I said, as we drove north to Hagerstown.

"Mmm."

"We need to go to grief counseling."

"Not now," said my mother, rolling her head toward the window.

"Not now as in 'I don't want to talk about it now?' or 'I'm not ready to go to grief counseling?'"

"Both," said my mother.

I gritted my teeth, thinking *I walked right into that one.*

"I'll go with you," I said. "Tasha will come, too. The three of us can go together."

"I don't see the point," said my mother. "I just want to block it all out."

"That's exactly the point," I said, bothered. "Blocking out your feelings is unhealthy. You need to deal with them. Get them out in the open."

"You're right," said my mother.

"We all miss Dad," I said.

"But I can't bear the thought of talking about my feelings with a stranger."

Now *she* was being selfish. "Mom—please," I said. "Do it for me."

I waited for her to say something. Anything. But there was a prolonged silence. It was all I could do to focus on my driving, but even that was hard. The sky was bleak, and the landscape blackened by snow that had been pummeled with exhaust fumes.

"Okay," said my mother. "I'll go."

"Thank you."

I should have felt triumphant, but instead I felt drained, fighting my own feelings of grief. *Just keep driving*, I thought as we barreled north. *Get the writing desk, and keep moving forward.*

WHEN WE ARRIVED at the warehouse in the middle of nowhere, my mother woke up with the abruptness of the engine shutting off. She squinted at the building.

"I'll wait in the car," she said, and flopped back on the headrest.

"Okay. I'll be right back." I raced toward the warehouse, cursing myself for having chosen a coat that was way too thin. I was still in warm LA-mode.

Inside the building, I approached a worker with a ruddy complexion who looked like he could hold his own in a brawl. I gave him my name and he punched it into a computer.

"Yup, it's here," he said. "Follow me."

Back outside, at a freestanding wood pallet, he uncrated my writing desk. I got all excited, running a hand over the dark wood table with its beautiful, clean lines, checking every crevice for signs of damage. There were no nicks or scratches.

"Looks great," I said.

"Want some help loading it into the car?"

"Please." I opened the trunk of the old Mercedes. The desk wasn't heavy, but it was awkward for one person to carry, especially a petite fifty-year-old.

We set the desk upside down in the trunk, with the legs sticking up too far for the lid to close all the way. The worker went and got a piece of rope, and then tied down the trunk.

"That should do it," he said. "But you best put your flashers on while you're driving."

I took his advice, setting off slowly for North Bethesda with Mom "flaked out." I could barely see out the rear window, the view cut off by the opened trunk. I hoped it didn't start snowing or raining. The beach blanket I had covered the desk with wouldn't protect it from the elements.

A misty rain began to fall as I exited highway 270. Five minutes later I pulled into our garage.

"Mom," I whispered. "We're home." She had slept the whole way.

I unlocked the basement door. My heart felt split in two; half of it overjoyed at reclaiming my treasured desk, and the other half despondent at my mother's ongoing inertia. After she went inside, out of earshot, I called Tasha and replayed the painstaking, grief-counseling conversation.

"I'm sorry you had to go through that," said Tasha. "But at least she's on board."

"We need to keep pushing her," I said. "All of us. Not just me."

Tasha told me that she would look at her schedule and set up a counseling session at Montgomery Hospice, a nonprofit organization in Maryland that offered bereavement counseling services. I didn't have to look at my calendar. I knew it was wide open, and counseling was a high priority.

IN THE NEXT FEW DAYS I went into overdrive, intent on finding a way to generate an income. But I was adamant about avoiding the sort of uninspiring work I'd done in the past to make ends meet. Fortunately, I wasn't in the position of having to simply *make ends meet,* because we had come to a family agreement that I would be given two thousand dollars per month to cover my fixed expenses: student loan payments, car insurance, and the minimum payment on two maxed-out credit cards. On the one hand, I was mortified to be receiving financial assistance from my mother at this stage of my life. On the other, the arrangement seemed fair since, upon moving in with her, I had taken over running the house and I'd become my mother's chauffeur. I was also filling her prescriptions at CVS.

Add-ons crept in.

"While you're there, can you pick up some nail polish remover for me?" my mother would say. Or, "Can you pick up a pair of stockings?"

Wandering the aisles of CVS, I would think, *Size B panty hose… did she say taupe or beige? Control Top or freestyle?*

I would have done all of these things for free, but the reality was, I needed the money, and my mother could afford to pay me. Humiliating as it was, I kept telling myself it was a fair trade-off: after dangling by a thread financially, I now had a reprieve from endless worrying. But I couldn't rely on my mother's generosity forever, nor did I want to; my pride wouldn't allow it. I wanted to stand on my own two feet financially.

DETERMINED TO MAKE the most of my set-up, I e-mailed Tasha for the name and phone number of the woman I'd met at my father's forty-day memorial service. I remembered her quick wit, but had blanked-out on most everything else, and wanted to set up a lunch meeting to discuss my idea from a few weeks earlier: to develop a reality TV show with my sister's friend (named Callie, I finally learned) as the host. There was also the anti-aging business that I had started in LA and let languish after my father's death. I wasn't keen on jumping back into it, but I had to keep every income-producing option on the table. I decided to try growing my business one person at a time. If I could just add one or two distributors to my team in the next few weeks, or sell some of the products to bring in a bit of income. But who would I call? Who did I know anymore in DC?

I turned to Tasha once again. She fed me all kinds of leads: people from the church, a real estate agent friend, even the neighborhood newsletter writer. I was grateful. Then again, I knew my sister would do anything to keep me in DC indefinitely, because that would take the pressure of caring for our mother off her. But I also knew her wish for me to succeed was sincere, and that I needed to start making money, which meant tapping into every resource I had.

Then my high school friend Lucy called. She was the one who had gotten me into "the beauty business" in the first place, signing me up as a distributor after I'd come up empty looking for work all up and down the West Coast. I had hoped to make use of my master's degree, working in the field of public diplomacy, but I gave up on that pipe dream within weeks of graduation. The recession was in full swing. Lucy gave me her pitch and I pored over the company specs, tried their products (which actually worked), and threw myself into a new career. But after four months of smiling and dialing, I'd earned less than a thousand dollars in commissions.

Technically, it was up to Lucy as my sponsor to help me grow the business.

"I'll be in New York next month," she said, calling soon after I arrived east. "I can make a detour to Bethesda, and we can work the phones together."

"My mother would love to see you," I said. "But we have to work."

"Of course!" said Lucy, getting all revved up. "We can introduce people to the business model, and do some product demos. I already called Amy Navinsky. She's going to invite people over to her house."

"Amy Navinsky?" I said, nearly dropping the phone. "I haven't heard that name in ages." This was another high school friend (more like an acquaintance), apparently still living in Maryland.

"She married Jeremy Winkleman," said Lucy.

"Oh?" These names from the seventies were coming at me way too fast. I couldn't picture Amy in my head. And I couldn't recall anything about Jeremy except that he grew pot in his backyard, and always struck me as being effeminate.

"Well," said Lucy, "two kids later he discovers he's gay, and they get divorced."

Bingo.

"Amy's not working," Lucy went on. "She's been out of the work force for years. Hello! Busy raising kids! And she really needs the money because Jeremy's screwing her on the alimony.

Boy, did he ever turn out to be a *schmuck*. Anyway she loves beauty products, but she's using crap stuff like Neutrogena."

"That's not so bad, is it?"

"Jana, our products are so much better! Come on. You know that."

It seemed like she was thinking twice as fast as me, and with a lot more conviction. I felt shaky. Did I have the stamina for the business? Physical energy was one thing, but you needed emotional energy for sales—the passion of a true believer. I scrounged around for my old notes, to start practicing my script. The one I'd used *ad nauseam* with "prospects" on the phone.

DURING MY FRENZY of unpacking and organizing, I noticed myself falling into a pattern when the house phone rang.

"Will you get that?" my mother would say, cloaked in grief.

By now more than two months had passed since my father's death, but my mother was still too upset about it to risk answering the phone; inevitably, the callers wanted to reminisce about Dad, which intensified her pain. It angered me that the force of her grief could have such a debilitating effect on my mother. The mom I'd grown up with was Xena the Warrior Phone Queen. Pity the pour soul on the other end of the line when she called to report a problem with a defective product of any kind.

"This is Mrs. Helen P. Panarites," she would say, straightaway, "and I would like to speak with the manager of your department."

Polite but firm was her style, and there was no point wasting time with the front line personnel. The higher-ups were the ones who could fix the situation.

It broke my heart to see my mother now, shrinking from the phone. At the same time, fielding the calls on her behalf was emotionally draining, and made me feel like a personal secretary. I answered the phone anyway, suffering enough for both of us.

"I'm so sorry about your father," the caller would say. "He was such a wonderful man."

"Thank you." Yes, my father was wonderful. I couldn't argue with that.

"Tell me, how is your mother doing?"

"Not great, but she's hanging in there."

Hanging in there. Clichés were made for conversations like this. Because honestly, who wanted to hear the gory details? Did anyone really want to know that my once dazzling, unbreakable mother was now sleeping away her days, at times not even bothering to bathe?

"It must be so difficult. She and your dad did everything together."

"Yes…" I felt a catch in my throat. Just when I was on an upswing, rebuilding my life.

"Was he sick? I'm sorry, it's just—well he seemed so healthy. Always smiling and in good spirits."

"Well, no, he wasn't outwardly sick," I said, seconds away from crying, "but he had a bubble on his ascending aorta. It burst, and he had a heart attack."

"Just like that. How awful."

"Yes. Uh… I'll tell my mother you called."

"Please do. Are you here for long, Jana, or are you intending to go back to Los Angeles?"

Why was I still on the phone? "I'm living with Mom for now," I said. Nothing more. Nip it in the bud.

"Oh, that's wonderful. And what will you do here?"

"I don't know yet." Heart palpitations. Insecurity spiking. "I'm sorry, but I have to go. I'll tell Mom you called."

"Thank you. And good luck to you, Jana."

Over and over again. Dragged back mercilessly to those awful first days after my father's death.

Upon receiving the phone messages, my mother would say, "That's so nice that she called." And then, matter-of-factly, she would add, "Her husband gets dialysis treatments twice a week." Or, "Her husband died six months before your dad. We're both widows now."

Wild-eyed from so much talk of ruination, I instituted a policy of refusing to answer the phone unless I could see from the caller ID that it was one of my sisters, or my sister-like cousin Margo, or my aunt—although at times even calls from Thea felt like falling into a vat of quicksand, because she, too, was depressed that Dad was gone, and needed an ear for her lamentations.

"Let it go into voice mail," I started saying whenever the house phone rang, and my mother asked if I would answer it.

Friends called to take her out to lunch, but my mother could barely even get to the phone.

"What if it's important?" she said.

"You can answer it." I was unnerved at how fast I'd gone from being patient with my mother to sounding peevish. But a tough-love strategy was critical to encourage her to connect with the outside world.

"It's usually for you, anyway," I added.

"But it may be someone I don't want to talk to," said my mother.

"Mom, that's why we have caller ID."

When my mother did answer the phone, I heard her say repeatedly, urgently: "I'm not accepting it," or "It's so hard," or "I feel like I'm living a nightmare"—phrases that hung in the air for days like motes of dust that never clear.

Then, in a softer tone (just loud enough for me to hear) she would say, "But Jana's here, and I'm so grateful for that," which made me feel loved and appreciated, yet also frighteningly aware that it was up to me to keep her emotionally propped up. Because who else was there to do it? My sisters called to check in, but they weren't in the M.A.S.H. unit like me, gutting it out with Mom.

It's part of the trade-off, I kept telling myself. *You chose to do this.*

What really threw me off was my mother's new habit of watching TV. I guessed it was an outlet for her grief, but it was completely out of character. The mother I knew had zero interest in the television. She was too busy reading or writing, or planning her next dinner party. But now I often found her watching TV in total darkness, leading me to think she'd been there all day.

"Didn't you watch that yesterday?" I asked, coming upon her one day (or was it night?). I knew I'd seen the same scene a day earlier. What I didn't know was that my mother's favorite shows were rerun on multiple channels from one day to the next.

"I don't remember," my mother said.

Her response troubled me, but I refused to see her forgetfulness as dementia, or God forbid: Alzheimer's. I told myself that during the first screening she simply hadn't been paying attention.

My mother had a preference for crime shows, and was a devoted *Law & Order* viewer. The entire franchise was acceptable, from the original courtroom drama with Sam Waterston to the *SVU* and *Criminal Intent* spin-offs. She got a kick out of the quirky acting style of Vincent D'Onofrio (*Criminal Intent*), and thought Christopher Meloni (*SVU*) was cute. I admired both actors, but when my mother told me Ice-T was her favorite, it was a game changer. The former gangsta rapper turned NYPD detective (*SVU*) couldn't have been further from her life experience.

"What is it that you like about Ice-T?" I asked my Canadian-born mother, Miss Manners devotee, and curator of my (unasked for, but accepted) Tiffany Shell & Thread silver pattern.

"Nothing gets by him," she said, shaking her head in awe.

Did she feel duped by my father's sudden death? Did it *get by* my mother?

I wondered if I would ever get used to this new Mom, and her unprecedented behaviors. I wanted the old Mom back. With this one, I was flying blind. I kept telling myself *trust your instincts, focus on keeping her safe*. I told myself I could navigate in the dark as if trained in instrumentation. It seemed that the life I had led—of thinking fast on my feet amid countless setbacks—had prepared me for this moment. But I knew deep down this would be the ultimate test of my mettle.

EIGHT DAYS AFTER arriving home, I felt organized enough to take a break from my punishing schedule. Things were looking up: the house was in order and I'd set up a few meetings. Tasha had scheduled a family grief-counseling session for two weeks from now. In my mind the session couldn't come fast enough. In the meantime, I employed another form of family therapy: opening a bottle of wine and coaxing my mother off the couch.

"Do you want to play Scrabble?" I asked, entering the family room late on a Friday afternoon.

"That would be nice," said my mother, eyes fluttering open from her horizontal position.

"I know we have a board around here somewhere. The question is, where?"

"I think it's in the TV cabinet," said my mother, pulling herself up off the couch.

My father had designed the white cabinet, another of his architectural flourishes. I bent at the knees, clasped the Lucite doorknobs, and opened the lower nook. A sudden sorrow shot through me. Inside the nook were VHS tapes I had given to my father one Christmas back in the eighties: *Young Frankenstein* and *A Night at the Opera*. His sense of humor ran the gamut, from the Marx Brothers to Falstaff. I wiped my eyes, retrieved the Scrabble board, and quickly closed the cabinet. Now I really needed a glass of wine.

My mother and I moved into the kitchen, where I pulled a bottle of Malbec out of the wine cooler built into the island counter (another Dad design).

"Not too much for me," said my mother, as I poured her a glass of wine.

She shook the bag of Scrabble tiles and pulled out a letter, clasping it to her chest as if I might grab it out of her hand.

I picked a tile, showed her the letter M, and she unveiled her letter G.

"Beat you," said my mother.

"Not yet," I said. "Pick your tiles."

She reached into the soft bag. My knee bounced under the table as I watched my mother pluck seven tiles from the bag and arrange them on the table—face up, for me to see.

"Is the Zoloft helping you?" I asked, thinking of my own bouts of despair.

"No," said my mother. "I'm still depressed."

"Well, it's not supposed to eliminate *all* your feelings. You wouldn't want that anyway."

My mother looked at me with raised eyebrows, as if she wouldn't mind it at all.

"You have an appointment soon with Dr. Post," I said. "We'll ask her about other options."

"I like her so much," said my mother.

Maybe she came in pill form. I was determined to boost my mother's spirits, not just for her sake, but mine. I was an optimist by nature, but I wasn't a Pollyanna, and I feared falling into my mother's pit of depression as well. If that happened we'd both be sunk: I wouldn't have the energy needed to run the house, and care for my mother or myself. I would just have to fit more Scrabble games with Mom into my schedule. *But that could hamper your career plans,* I thought. I told myself I was being paranoid, and that I enjoyed playing Scrabble just as much as my mother did. I could find an hour here and there to play the game. That sparked another spirit-boosting thought: as long as my mother was spending so much time in front of the television, why not rent some DVDs and we could watch movies together—one of my favorite pastimes. Much of my childhood had been spent watching classics like *The Killers* and *Double Indemnity*.

"What would you think about buying a bigger television?" I said.

"Well… where would we put it?" said my mother.

"To the right of the fireplace."

My mother grimaced. "That would make it the focal point of the room."

"Now you sound like Dad."

"He was so fussy about things like that," my mother said, on the verge of tears.

I braced myself for an outburst. "He was," I said. "So… what do you think?"

"About…."

"Getting a new television. They're not too expensive."

"Okay," said my mother, brightening, with effort. "I guess that would be good."

Pleased, I watched as she put the word *SAP* on the board.

"Pretty lame," my mother said dully. "How many points is that?"

"You tell me," I said, thinking she should do the math, to keep her brain humming.

"I'll have to put on my glasses," said my mother, searching the area. "Have you seen them?"

"No. Please don't tell me you lost your glasses again."

"Well, they're here somewhere."

"I'll add it up." I wanted to keep the game moving. "One, one, three, times two since it's a double score… ten points." I wrote it down.

We continued playing, and the board became littered with my mother's three-letter words *(SAP, TEA, TIN)*, offset by my four- to seven-letter creations.

"Look outside," I said, fixated on the sheets of snow ripping through the air, the child in me filled with wonder. Happy memories of Christmases when my father was still alive.

"Will you accept *RAD*?" said my mother, turning to the French doors, halting.

"Isn't it beautiful?"

"I hope it doesn't last." My mother returned to the game. "Will you let me do it?"

"What's a *RAD*?" I said, eyeing the letter *R* in her hand.

"A unit of measurement."

"Huh?"

"Look it up," she said with a shrug.

How could my mother know what a *rad* was, and not remember to take her pills each day? "Go for it," I said, clueless.

An hour later, we finished our Scrabble game and moved into the living room. I made a fire in the fireplace while the television played uninterrupted news coverage of the snowstorm. The weatherman assured us we were in for a major dumping, but reporters always exaggerated, so I kept it in perspective. It all went out the window when I checked the backyard. The patio furniture was barely visible, swamped by white fluff.

All of a sudden the TV snapped to black and the lights in the room cut out.

"Shit." I went in search of a flashlight, stopping to look out the powder room window.

"Are the streetlights out?" I heard my mother saying.

The street was black, like peering into the maw of a whale. "I can't see a thing," I said, astounded.

A flood of memories ran through my mind of the countless times I'd called my parents from California and heard they were in the midst of a power outage. "We called Pepco an hour ago," my father would say. "Who knows what they're doing out there."

I went to the hall closet and retrieved an industrial-strength flashlight. Back in the family room, I placed the beaming flashlight upside down on the glass coffee table. Light bounced off the ceiling and cast a yellow veil in the room, like an illuminated tent at night.

I picked up the telephone and listened for a dial tone. Silence. No house lights, no streetlights, no landline. I felt anxious. This wasn't a blown fuse. That would have been an easy fix. The situation felt more ominous, like end times.

I called Tasha on my BlackBerry. "Do you guys have power?"

"Nope. We're in the dark," said Tasha. "How's Mom doing?"

"Better than me." I wiped my damp forehead, telling myself the house would retain heat for at least twelve hours, and we had plenty of firewood. All manner of heavy blankets were upstairs. "Call me later to check in, okay? I'm not used to this."

"Welcome home!" said Tasha.

"That's not even funny. Talk to you later." I hung up, sat on the edge of the couch, and stared at the flames in the fireplace.

"I guess we won't be having the lamb chops," my mother said forlornly.

I got up and threw another log on the fire, steeling my nerves, tamping down my hunger. There had to be a way to cook the lamb chops, even without electricity. *Of course*, I thought.

I rushed past my mother, into the kitchen, and came back with the preseasoned chops and a grate from the oven. I set the grate on the fireplace logs, and began grilling the lamb over the flames.

"How about that," my mother said, shaking her head.

I left the meat on the grate, and returned to the kitchen to make a salad.

"Let me know if anything explodes," I called out.

Thirty minutes later, we toasted our candlelit dinner.

"This is wonderful," my mother said—and for a moment I believed she was happy.

WHEN I AWOKE the next day, my eyes felt tingly. Everything around me was bleached out, as if I'd slept in a padded cell. The white duvet bled into the white walls. Through the window I saw white outdoors. I swung my legs off the bed. The air felt cooler and crisper than last night. I flipped on a light switch. Nothing. We were still without power. What time was it, anyway? I checked the battery-powered clock: 10:30. No power for over twelve hours. *That's not good*, I thought. But maybe it wouldn't last. After all that down time, it was possible the restoration of our electricity was at hand. I crept down the hallway, past my father's closed bathroom door, and went downstairs.

I cracked open the front door. A shimmering ledge of snow appeared at my knees. I looked up, surveying the accumulation in the neighborhood.

"Oh my God."

Cars were buried in powdery white mounds. Tree branches sagged under massive sleeves of snow. Bands of low-slung, ice-covered electrical wires smiled between foamed-up telephone poles.

Where's Pepco? I thought, hands shaking. *Where are the snow plows?* The street hadn't even been plowed. I felt my cheeks getting cold, and closed the door.

I moved into the formal dining room and opened the drapes in front of the sliding glass doors. The backyard was a sugary white carpet. A few feet in front of me was a long strip of aluminum, half-buried in the snow. I glanced up and then stepped back. The aluminum strip was the gutter. The snowstorm had severed it off the roof. I had to call someone to have it reattached, or it would lay on the ground forever. Standing there, I realized I was now the man of the house.

I went into the family room and stared at the heap of snow on our driveway, like a dog fixated on a squirrel. That was another project I'd have to attend to. *So, you'll get some exercise,* I told myself, steering myself away from negative thoughts while trying to recall the last time I'd shoveled snow. What was it—thirty years ago? No point rushing into that one. For the time being I would carve a path from the front door to the curb in case of an emergency.

Just then I remembered there had already been one fatal emergency in the house, and that my mother was eighty years old. I dashed up to her bedroom.

"Mom," I said, tiptoeing inside. "Are you okay?"

"Yes," said the voice beneath the blanket. "Do we have power?"

"Not yet."

"Oh, dear."

"I'm going outside to shovel the walkway," I said. "I'll get a fire going after that."

"Wear a heavy jacket. Put on a scarf, and a wool hat."

"I will," I said, feeling like I was twelve years old again.

Back downstairs, I snagged a bottle of water from the fridge and put on my father's thermal, quilted jacket, suiting up as directed. I located boots of the kind that weren't among my LA footwear collection, found a shovel in the garage, and came back upstairs. The biggest snowstorm to hit the US in nearly ninety years had arrived on our doorstep.

Beyond the front door the snow was thigh high, piles of glistening white in all directions under a blanket of bright sun. I dug my way down the walkway, furiously, with no time to waste in the freezing air, and then stopped halfway down the walk after heaving too much too quickly. I took a swig of the bottled water. Under the glare of sunlight the house seemed spectacular, like the mansion in *Gone with the Wind*. I thought about how my father had always corrected me when I referred to it as *your house*. "It's your house, too," he would say.

But I never accepted his claim. I hadn't lived there for ages, and felt detached from our family home. It was my father's achievement, not mine: the stakes he put down in suburbia. But the longer I stared at the house, the more I saw it in a new light. Maybe I wasn't the owner, but by virtue of my father's absence, and my mother's grief-stricken state, I was the one responsible for keeping the house intact. It was part of my father's legacy, something I had to preserve.

With a new sense of purpose, I threw myself back into the task at hand, sweating in the cold as I heaved up chunks of snow. Day gave way to night, followed by foraging for unspoiled food. By the time power was restored to our neighborhood, my mother and I had endured twenty-one hours without electricity. I don't recall how we occupied our time, but I know we ran out of firewood.

THE NEXT MORNING we had another power outage. By then the charming winter wonderland had morphed into an annoying, cruel joke. In my battle with Mother Nature, a gauntlet had been thrown down. I called Tasha from my newly recharged BlackBerry for an update on her end.

"We're back on line," said Tasha. "And we have firewood."

"Can one of you come and get us?" I said. It was time to evacuate.

George picked us up, and we settled in for a sleepover. My mother endured it with aplomb, as if the record-breaking snowfall was a mere inconvenience. I guess after my father's death nothing could rattle her. But I was anxious to get past the disruption and get back on track with my career plans. With so many shops and businesses shut down, I had already been forced to push back my lunch meeting with Callie.

We returned to the house to find it was operational. But this wasn't exactly a cause for celebration, because now the cleanup crew had to do its job, and that cleanup crew was me. The snow removal squads (enterprising kids in the neighborhood) were overbooked. I layered up and took to the driveway, once again heaving aside squares of snow like giant pieces of cake.

"Not like California is it?" called out our neighbor Betty, a salt-of-the-earth, Ma Kettle type.

"Nope," I shouted.

"How's your Mom doing?"

"Hanging in there," I said, tired of the question. Tired of my own stupid answer.

"Tell her we're thinking about her," said Betty. "Let us know if you need anything."

"Thank you." I appreciated her kind words. I looked up just briefly, determined to finish my task. I had to keep going or I'd never get to the end.

Four hours later I stomped at the ground, shaking the snow off my boots, aching, but satisfied. The driveway was clear, the worst of the snowstorm over. I went back inside and checked my e-mail. One of them was from the Montgomery County Emergency Communications System. It read: "Another major winter storm expected tomorrow with 10–20" of snowfall possible."

I almost started crying.

A WEEK LATER the main roads were passable enough to drive on, and even if they hadn't been, I would have gone begging door-to-door in search of chains to put on the tires. It was time for the grief-counseling session. I'd put so much effort into convincing my mother to go, it was time for the payoff. Finally we could speak frankly about the effects of my father's death.

I put on a coat and went to collect my mother, sacked out on the couch.

"Let's go, Mom," I said, like a drill sergeant. "We're meeting Tasha at twelve-thirty."

"Is that the counseling thing?" she asked, draping a hand over her eyes.

"Yes."

"Do I have to go?" said my mother.

"Yes. You promised to do this. You already committed to it." I stood stock still, telling myself not to give in to her objections.

"Come on, Mom," I pleaded. "Please get up."

To speed things along, I brought out a black-and-white checked coat for her to wear.

"I know you'll get something out of this," I said, softening at the sight of my mother struggling just to pull herself up off the couch. "We'll do something fun afterward."

"Can we make popcorn?" she asked. Bargaining, like a child.

"Sure." I threw her coat over my arm, held out a hand. "Let me help you." She took my hand, straightening up. "Does your back hurt?"

"Terribly," said my mother.

"Did you put on a Lidoderm patch?"

"A what?"

"The medicated patches Dr. Shin prescribed." I felt my chest tightening, and exhaled to steady my nerves. Gently, I lifted the back of her shirt, exposing her bare back.

"What are you doing?" she said, flinching.

"Can you reach around with your arms?"

"Yes, but—"

"Okay, so you can put on the patches." I dropped her coat on the couch. "Mom, you have to take care of yourself," I added, in a harsher tone. "I can't do everything for you."

"You're right." She sat on the couch, all used up.

"Don't put on your coat yet," I said.

I hurried upstairs, grabbed a Lidoderm patch from the hall closet, and cut it open. I sped downstairs and back into the family room.

"Turn around, please." I unpeeled the patch. Laid the jellied square against her lower back.

"Ooh!" My mother jerked her hips forward. "That's so cold!"

"I'm sorry," I said, wincing, lowering her shirt. "But I bet you feel better."

"It does feel nice," she admitted. "But you have to slow down."

"I can't. We don't have time."

I held up her coat and she got into it, then I wrapped a scarf around my mother's neck. I pulled the gloves out of her pockets and handed them to her, my blood level rising. *Breathe,* I thought. *Take a long breath.*

FOR A LONG TIME no one said anything, which was ironic given how gung-ho I'd been to get us all in the room. But now I felt tongue-tied and drowsy, as if I were coming out of a coma. Where was I? The air smelled sweet, like perfumed wood. Was someone burning incense? I couldn't see any wisps of smoke. Actually, the room was so dimly lit I couldn't see much of anything.

I made out Tasha across from me and my mother on my left in a brocaded chair. I felt the edge of a coffee table at my knees. Boxes of tissues were strategically placed near Victorian-era reproduction tables. And there was the social worker, a thirtyish, black woman named Awa.

"Would anyone like to say how they're feeling?" said Awa.

"Dad was a central figure in all of our lives," Tasha said. "So... it's hard."

My eyes swelled with tears at the words *Dad was*. Past tense.

"I miss him," I said, reaching for a tissue. "But I think he would be happy to know I moved back east."

Awa nodded. Close to whispering, she said, "Helen... how are you feeling?"

My mother shook her head. I couldn't tell whether she was crying behind her tinted glasses.

"Sometimes it helps to talk about the good memories," Awa added.

Please say something, I thought, gaping at my mother like she was a Virgin Mary statue and I was waiting for the miracle of a tear falling down her cheek.

"It's so hard for me to see my mother like this," I said.

My mother gave me a brief look, and then raised her eyebrows at Awa, as if to say *I'm sorry, but being a widow is all consuming.* There was something haughty about her expression.

"Peter and I went to South Africa," my mother said, as an offering. "We saw the giraffes. And the cheetahs—those were my favorites." She paused, distressed. "I never got to say goodbye."

That's good, I thought, *keep talking.* But the deafening silence continued. Things weren't going at all as I'd planned. Why wasn't my mother making more of an effort?

"One of the hardest things," I said, "is—is seeing Mom sleep so much."

"Well," said Awa, straightening, "prolonged sleep is a common grief response."

I almost choked on the word *prolonged*. Pouring myself a cup of water, I drained it in one gulp. As I set down the cup, Awa gave me a tranquil smile. It would take years for me to achieve anything close to her Zen-like level of self-command.

"How long does the sleeping last?" I said.

"The road ahead could be endless," said Awa. "But there's no need to panic."

It sounded like a *haiku*. "Can you explain that?"

"Certainly," Awa said. She drew two vertical lines on a blank piece of paper, creating three columns on the page. In the far left column she wrote OLD REALITY.

"This column on the left represents life before your father died," said Awa. "Happier times, when life was mostly predictable."

My mother was barely paying attention. Bothered, I watched as Awa wrote NEW REALITY on the far right side of the paper.

"This column on the right," she said, "represents life without your father, a scenario that has yet to be defined."

Old reality, new reality—I had a bad feeling about this. What was in the middle?

"This new reality will be different from the old one," said Awa, "but not necessarily joyless."

Another *haiku*. "What does the new reality look like?" I said. "It has to be better than where we are now."

"It will be," said Awa. "Because where you are now," she continued, "is right here." She poked at the middle of the page and wrote UNKNOWN. "In this gray area."

"Wow," said Tasha. "That is so interesting."

I gaped in recognition at the drawing in Awa's hands. It was the classic myth paradigm, straight out of *The Hero with a Thousand Faces*, one of my favorite books. The middle area was "the road of trials," the great unknown where the hero faces a series of hardships and unforeseen challenges that lead to a place of wisdom—like the *NEW REALITY* before us, that had yet to be defined. At least now I had a familiar framework to work with. And yet that *UNKNOWN* column on the paper was disturbingly wide.

When the fifty-minute session ended, I embraced Awa as if we were old friends. She was the most serene person I had ever met. She hugged my mother, gave me her business card, and said to call any time.

"This summer we'll be offering group sessions for widows," Awa said, glancing at my mother. "I can send you some materials."

My mother nodded, but I didn't hold out much hope for that one, given how much prodding it took to get her to this session, and the fact that she'd barely said a word.

"I have to get back to work," said Tasha. "I'll talk to you guys later."

I watched her dash off, a little resentful and more than a little jealous—not just that she had a job, but that she could go back to the working world and forget about our father's death for a while. I couldn't escape his dark shadow. Our house was filled with Dad mementos and the bleakness of his shattered wife.

I automatically circled around to my mother's left side, and she hooked onto my arm. Whenever we walked together, my mother preferred to have me on her left side. I never asked why. I just fell into position and waited for her to lock on.

"That wasn't so bad, was it?" I said.

"It was okay," said my mother.

"Would you go again?"

"Maybe yes, maybe no," she said, giving me hope, but holding herself to nothing. "That lady was nice," my mother added. "How did we find her?"

"Through a work friend of Tasha's."

My mother shook her head in amazement, getting into the old Mercedes.

"These services that we had no idea existed," she said, "until"—*go on*, I thought, *you can do it*—"until your Dad died."

I shut her door, swallowing hard. *Dad died*. I was still getting used to those words. I had tripped on them, stifled them, and substituted them with the tried and true euphemism "he passed away." Whenever I said "my father died," I felt like a ventriloquist speaking through a doll. I imagined my lips on wooden hinges, clucking mechanically for the audience at hand. *My. Father. Died.* He had loomed so large in my life, that to say he was dead felt like an act of deception.

5
Sold Out

Three months since Dad's death.

"OH MY GOSH!" Lucy reached out to hug me, dragging her suitcase over the asphalt in front of Union Station. "It's so good to see you! How's your mom? How are you? Can you believe we're both in DC again?"

Scattered but wonderful Lucy. She was smart and kind-hearted, the sort of person who would call Animal Rescue if she saw a dog lying on the side of the road. Our lives had gone in opposite directions after high school. Lucy had gotten married, moved to Georgia, and now had two teenagers, whereas I had remained single, bouncing between New York and LA.

"Hi, great to see you, too," I said, eyeing the fat lady cop behind Lucy waving her hand at me like a windmill. "Get in," I added. "I'm about to get ticketed."

Before I could pull away from the curb, Lucy was calling the guy above her on the leadership ladder—checking in, grabbing tips, and jabbering on about how the DC market was completely untapped where our anti-aging products were concerned.

"Oh, yeah," she said, "We're gonna rock this town!"

"Modest goals," I said, straining to find the train station exit. "Remember, you're only here for two days." Where was Massachusetts Avenue? I was on a roundabout, circling a United Nations-like row of flags.

"Do you know where you're going?" Lucy asked, twisting around in her seat.

"Kind of."

"Don't you have a GPS?"

"No."

"Jana, you have to get a GPS," Lucy said.

"I found it." I turned up Massachusetts Avenue. "We're good."

"Why don't you have a GPS?"

"Because I don't need one," I said. "I look things up. Geez. Does everything have to be figured out for us? Can't we use our brains once in a while? And what's wrong with getting lost?"

"Okay..." Lucy said.

"Sorry. I'm a little stressed out. My mother's home alone and I always feel guilty leaving her there. But she's looking forward to seeing you, so that's good."

"Girard." Lucy jerked toward her phone. "Yes, I'm still here."

It was noon by the time we got back to suburbia, thankfully, without any directional cock-ups.

"Gosh," Lucy said, wandering through the house, "I haven't been here in ages."

"Not since my high school graduation party, right?"

Nearly the entire class of 1977 had showed up that night. The noise in the backyard had driven one of the neighbors to call the cops. My father had coolly explained to the officers that it was all under control; we were just a happy bunch of high school seniors, letting off steam. That was my dad.

"Mrs. Panarites!" said Lucy, cutting into the family room, arms outstretched.

My mother rolled off the couch and Lucy gave her a big hug.

"Call me Helen," she demurred. "Please. It's so nice to see you."

"I'm so sorry about your husband," Lucy said.

"Thank you," said my mother. "Would you like something to eat?"

"Oh, no, I'm fine."

I faced Lucy, tense. "Let's go into the kitchen and talk about what we're going to do."

"Sure. Do you want to come sit with us?" she asked my mother.

"I think we should work alone," I said. "No offense, Mom. Do you want me to find a program for you to watch?"

My mother shook her head. "I'll just lie down."

"Or you could do the crossword puzzle," I said. "It's good for the brain."

"Maybe later," said my mother, returning to the couch. "You girls do your work."

"Why can't she sit with us?" said Lucy, as we went into the kitchen. "It will be good for her."

"Yes, but it will be bad for me," I said. "I need to focus, and my mother will be a distraction. We'll visit with her later."

"Sure, I get it," said Lucy, in a tone that suggested she didn't get it at all.

Why did I feel like the bad guy?

"It must so hard for her," Lucy said, "after being with your dad all those years."

"Yeah, it's tough." I was starting to lose the thread of why she was here, as if we were about to slide down the wormhole of grief.

"So. Would you like something to drink?" I said. "Seltzer? Diet Coke? Glass of wine?" Wine sounded good. But it was only noon. That was a bad sign.

"Diet Coke would be great," said Lucy, plopping down with her laptop, pulling a file out of her satchel. "I just have to call my daughter. I'll be quick."

"Speaking of wine," I said, "that networking event at Clyde's tonight starts at five o'clock."

I had heard about the event at Clyde's restaurant through a friend of Tasha's. It was the sort of thing I would have been comfortable attending alone when my father was alive, but since his death, the thought of pitching myself into a pack of strangers was terrifying, like going on a hundred blind dates at once.

Lucy argued on the phone with her daughter. "How will you get there? What other girls are going? What time does it end?" The world of a teenager was foreign to me, and hearing Lucy haggle with her daughter I was glad for it, because I already had my hands full with Mom. Living with an octogenarian was like having a grown-up toddler. My days went something like this:

1. Wake-up, go for walk to preserve sanity, return to the house before Mom wakes up in case she falls down the stairs.

2. Make coffee, leave enough for Mom to consume (whenever she wakes up) because she still doesn't know how to use the coffee machine.

3. Open slot on Mom's pill rack to day of week (S-M-T-W-T-F-S), set rack in plain sight on the kitchen counter with glass of water to guarantee she takes pills.

4. Call CVS to refill low prescriptions (pick up later in week; drop-off dry cleaning same day to save time).

5. Check calendar for Mom's appointments with doctor, dentist, etc. Wake her up as needed, take her to appointment, produce insurance cards from my wallet (where they live permanently), and pay attention in appointment because Mom won't.

6. Schedule follow-up appointment, enter in BlackBerry, set notification for one day in advance. Enter appointment on wall calendar or monthly planner if more than a month away.

7. Make work calls, check e-mails, take meetings, draft documents in and around appointments, checking in intermittently with Mom to make sure she hasn't lost her glasses or wedding band again, and is at least dressed for the day.

8. Check fridge, buy groceries as needed because Mom isn't driving (don't forget wine; pick up dry cleaning).

9. Capitulate to Mom's request to drive her to Macy's or CVS for girdle, bra, or shade of lipstick only she can identify.

10. Make dinner for both of us, clean up afterward, tee-up movie for us to watch on TV for entertainment and distraction from grief (if I'm staying in).

11. If I'm going out: worry about how long it's safe to leave Mom alone in the house.

12. Interrupt Mom when I overhear her say, "I'll give you the credit card number" on phone. Scold telemarketer for preying on a senior. Remind Mom not everyone is as honest as her.

13. Make plans to go out with a friend, to preserve sanity.

"Sorry about that," said Lucy, setting down her iPhone, rubbing her eyes. "Oy. She can be so annoying. But she's a good kid. Okay, where were we?"

The next two days were a blur of cold calling, in-person networking, and Lucy entertaining my mother while I served up food and drinks.

"She's a lovely girl," said my mother, when Lucy was out of the room. "So much energy."

"Is it exhausting for you?" I said.

"No, it's refreshing. Both you girls are such go-getters."

"I'll invite Toni over, too," I said, referring to the only other high school friend I kept in touch with. "Do you remember seeing her at the funeral?"

"No," said my mother. "That whole period is a fog."

I felt incapacitated myself, making cold calls with Lucy, saying things like: "This company has discovered something that will revolutionize skincare for the next fifty years. Have a look at this website, and I can help you build this business."

"Relax," said Lucy, when we got off the phone with her friend Amy, who had not, in fact, organized the product demo party as promised, and apparently had no intention of doing so. "You sound stiff. Remember, it's about educating people."

She was so much better at it than I was. I wondered if I was ever any good at my business to begin with. Or was it that I didn't care about it any more? The whole enterprise seemed more credible in LA, where selling anti-aging products was a no-brainer. But here in the land of think tanks and lawyers, looking twenty years old forever didn't seem to be a priority. I couldn't sell anyone anything. I was all sold out. Making my calls, all I could think about was my father lying in a box, and here I was reading from a script someone had come up with to fleece the masses with magic creams. Okay, maybe it wasn't that dodgy. But I couldn't fake what I didn't feel, and I wasn't feeling the words in the script. I felt sad and outside of my body. Disconnected from my mouth.

As for the networking event at Clyde's, Lucy thankfully took the lead, chatting up wheeler-dealers dressed in everything from mohair shirts over jeans, to suits and ties, and skirts with matching blazers. Bouncy music from the seventies blared out of the sound system—"Play that funky music, white boy!"—as we jostled around the crowded bar.

The level of unapologetic, in-your-face networking was dizzying. Heads nodded emphatically. Hands outlined shapes in the air, reached into pockets, and produced business cards.

I felt sluggish, like I was at the gym for the first time after eating doughnuts for a year. But then, after a second glass of wine, I felt like the fittest person in the room. My tongue loosened up, and I began to form questions. "What are you doing now? Do you enjoy it? Would you consider something else?"

When the event was over, I realized I had only survived the night because being around so many rabidly ambitious people was intoxicating, like being at a rave for entrepreneurs. The stories I heard were fascinating. Unfortunately, I was so busy listening, I forgot to promote my business. But I vowed to follow up with my new acquaintances because I did believe in our products, even if I wasn't very good at selling them.

6

The Odd Couple

Three months since Dad's death.

You would think that a breather was in order after Lucy left town, but the idea of slowing down didn't even occur to me. I was starting to get into a rhythm—a manic one, admittedly, but one that came naturally because I had my mother's boundless energy. Or I should say, the energy she had before my father died and which was now entirely absent. But I couldn't dwell on that. I had to stay positive and push ahead.

After I dropped off Lucy at Union Station, I found my way to downtown Bethesda and searched for Mon Ami Gabi, the restaurant Callie had chosen for us to meet at. I drove around in circles looking for the restaurant and a place to park amid the piles of snow and frosted-up windows. Finally, I found a parking spot, and doubled back toward the restaurant on foot.

As I was walking, I called my mother. She had promised to get out of bed soon after I left the house.

"Hi Mom, it's me," I said, dodging patches of ice on the sidewalk. "Are you up?"

"Sort of."

"What does that mean?"

"Well, I got up for some water," she said in a raspy voice, "but then I got back into bed. Do you get a dry mouth at night? It's awful. Last night I was at an art fair with your father."

Another dream, I thought, confused at first. "Mom, you promised to get out of bed. It's almost twelve-thirty."

"Oh… but the dream was so nice. We bought some ceramic pillars we didn't need, but we liked them so we got them anyway."

"Dr. Post wanted you to be up at nine," I said, craning my neck, searching for the restaurant.

"I don't feel like getting up."

"Well, it's feeding your depression," I said, annoyed by her indifference.

"But when I'm asleep I get to be with your father."

"But you're alive, Mom, and he's not."

"I know."

"Get up and take your pills. Call a friend or get on the exercise bike."

"I will."

"Please. If I come home and find you're still in bed, I'm going to be upset."

I got off the phone, mentally switching gears as I entered Mon Ami Gabi, barely registering the cozy bistro setting.

"Sorry I'm late," I said, plunking down across from Callie at a table for two. "It took me a while to get through traffic. And I kept getting lost."

"No problem," said Callie. "I'm always early. I'm paranoid about being late for client meetings."

I liked the sound of that. If we were going to work together, it was reassuring to know we both valued punctuality. I ordered a salad and got down to business.

"So here's my idea," I said. "I want to do a reality TV show around Greek food and culture. Visions of *Zorba* are dancing in my head, and the Greek, full-throttle approach to life. That's what I want to celebrate and share with our viewers."

"What a great idea," said Callie. "We could have so much fun with that."

"Having fun is the goal," I said. "Well—that and making money." I felt relaxed and confident, not at all the way I'd felt making cold calls and reading my wrinkle-reduction script.

"We could go behind the scenes at the hot Greek restaurants in town," Callie said. "I know most of the owners personally."

"What about the church ladies?" The church was the cradle of the Greek community, a casting director's jackpot.

"Oh yeah," Callie said. "You're talking about some very colorful characters there."

I imagined she could persuade a few of them to participate in our reality TV show. When I told Callie that my sister's neighbor was an executive at Discovery, and that we could probably get a meeting with her, she said, "Oh, I am *so* in. And I have ideas for other shows!"

"How do you feel about being on camera?"

"Are you kidding?" said Callie. "I grew up in Hollywood!"

I laughed. I couldn't help thinking what an odd pair we were. Callie seemed uncensored with a slapdash style, whereas I usually thought twice before speaking and was a stickler for organization. And she was married with three daughters, whereas I was single with a widow. But neither of us was exactly conventional. I thought our contrasting styles would be complementary.

"You need to start watching food shows," said Callie.

"I can do that," I said, on an upswing again.

I BEGAN MY RESEARCH, diving into the unfamiliar world of food shows like *Throwdown! with Bobby Flay*, *Chopped*, and *Anthony Bourdain's No Reservations*. I hadn't bought the new TV yet, but the shows were splashy enough for any size screen, and I roped my mother into the viewings so we could both get something out of them. While I analyzed the style and structure of the shows, Mom reveled in the light-hearted entertainment, which lightened the mood in our house.

"I would eat that," said my mother, considering a Flay-prepared omelet.

"The question is, would you cook it?"

"Probably not." She paused. "But you could cook it for me."

"Sure, because I have nothing better to do," I said, thinking *brass balls; that's the old Mom*. "I might make it for you if you got out of bed at a decent hour."

"Not a bad incentive," said my mother.

I cracked a smile, energized by the work, seeing my mother distracted from her grief.

But the more time I spent fleshing out the Greek show, the more I struggled with my skincare business. It wasn't for lack of effort; since Lucy's departure, I had called a handful of prospects, diligently keeping to a schedule as if it were Pledge Week at our house. But I couldn't convince anyone to join my distribution team or even try out the main product (a home spa treatment). I grew impatient and bored. Worse, the constant selling was bringing me down, and I was already fighting the blues, missing Dad.

His absence in our house seemed to claw at my throat. Straining to make calls from my bedroom, I would glance out the window and remember all the parties we'd had on the patio when Dad was alive, the footballs thrown on the lawn, and my incessant childhood pleading to install a pool in the vast field of grass ("We have a community pool," my father would say. "You can swim there."). From that vantage point, filled with bittersweet memories, it was all I could do to keep from crying (or laughing) at every objection I heard from my prospects on the phone.

Three of them who worked for competing skincare companies assured me they had the best products on the market. How could they all be right? And proving them wrong was so tedious. Not to mention that it was easier to catch lightning in a bottle than convince a woman to change her beauty products. Another prospect gave me the number of a stay-at-home mom with twins who might be persuaded to join my distribution team. I jotted down the number knowing I'd never make the call; there were only so many hours in the day, and I cared more about developing the Greek show, and getting my mother to all her appointments.

By now the two of us had settled into an "odd couple" routine based on our mutual goal of adjusting to life without Dad. While I spun in all directions, my mother mostly slept through her grief. We were two women with radically different life experiences, each resorting to instinct and letting fate decide the rest.

"What are you doing awake?" I murmured one night, glass of wine in hand, startled to see my pajama-clad mother descending the stairs as I was heading up. It must have been around 3 a.m.

"I can't sleep," she said.

"Me neither," I replied.

"I'm getting something to eat," said my mother.

"Don't forget to turn off the lights." Up the stairs I went as she continued downward. We were like souls lost in Purgatory.

At times the contrast in our ways of living became fodder for comic relief, which I sought at every turn as a weapon against my sorrow.

"Mom, I don't care what your bedroom looks like," I would say, parent-like, laughing at the absurdity of the situation. "Just please close your door."

Slacks, sweaters, dresses, and hosiery were strewn across her bedroom furniture like a sample sale at Barney's. My mother's bathroom resembled a hair salon at the peak of the weekend, littered with curlers, bobby pins, opened jars of creams, and uncapped tubes of lipstick.

"Your dad would have never let me get away with this," she said.

I admired her ability to call the mess for what it was. And then I realized it must have been taxing to live with someone as fastidious as my father. Her sloppiness struck me as much an act of liberation as a manifestation of her grief.

"Peter, would you zip me up?" she said, coming toward me one day. Frozen-faced, she added, "Did you hear what I just said?"

I was aghast. Being mistaken for my father—that was a first. I thought, *am I turning into Dad? Have I always been Dad?* I rethought my habits, cataloguing our similarities. I kept the kitchen counter spotless like my father, and was equally meticulous in other areas of my life. Both our wardrobes were pared down to the essentials and arranged in the closet with a military precision. But wasn't that simply because of the space limitations of every apartment I'd ever lived in? Wasn't pruning my wardrobe a matter of logistics?

Deductive reasoning pushed me in a new direction. What if I was now enabling my mother in the same way my father had, continuing the cycle of dependence?

7

What Do You Do?

Three-and-a-half months since Dad's death.

I BROUGHT THE MAIL into the kitchen, thrown by the sight of my mother in her bathrobe, eating breakfast at two in the afternoon. I still wasn't used to seeing her start her days so late.

"Anything interesting?" she said, eyeing the pile in my hands.

"Let's see." The lavender-colored envelope was addressed to my mother, but I opened it anyway and read the invitation aloud. "In Their Own Words. A literary luncheon featuring four Greek-American writers who will reflect on their craft, and provide insight into their work."

The writers listed were crime novelist George Pelecanos; sports writer Stefan Fatsos; children's book author Nick

Katsoris; and former CIA Director George Tenet, who had just published an autobiography. I turned the invitation in my mother's direction.

"It's a luncheon sponsored by the church," I said, "next Saturday at the Bethesda Country Club. Why don't you go?"

My mother eyed the invitation and went back to her *Washington Post*. "I'm in no mood to socialize."

"I think it would be good for you to get out of the house." I waited for a response, but my mother was absorbed in the newspaper.

"You didn't even read it," I said, frustrated, setting the invitation on the table.

My mother picked it up, read it for two seconds, and then dropped it onto the table as if to say, *there—satisfied?*

I should have known my mother wouldn't go to the luncheon on her own. She was used to doing everything with my father. She didn't even like eating alone.

"Are you leaving?" she said late one morning, as she came into the kitchen.

"Yes, I've already eaten." I tossed the sponge behind the faucet.

"You can still sit with me."

"No, I can't," I said, bothered. "I have to make some calls."

"Not even for a few minutes?"

"Mom, please. I'm trying to earn a living here."

My mother scowled. It seemed like she felt entitled to my companionship, as if now that my father was gone it was only logical that I should take his place at the table.

"Lots of people eat alone," I added.

"Believe me, I'm getting used to it," said my mother.

I shook my head.

As for the "In Their Own Words" literary luncheon, the thought of donning business casual on a Saturday morning was loathsome. But I did have a soft spot for George Pelecanos. I had met him in the early 1980s, and he'd read one my first screenplays. His words of praise inspired me to keep toiling away at my craft. Years later, I sent Pelecanos a letter telling him how much I enjoyed his novel *Shoedog*. He encouraged me to try my hand at a novel, arguing, "It's all yours… not like this screenplay business… and don't ever think you're not a writer because you've failed to sell your work. Keep writing; I know, I've given you that advice before. But do it anyway."

I reread the luncheon invitation. It would be fun to see Pelecanos again after all these years. I doubted he would remember me, but so what?

"What if I went with you?" I said to my mother. "You could write an article about it for the *Herald*. Didn't Dr. Post say it would be good for you to get back to your writing?"

My mother dropped her newspaper. I knew the mention of Dr. Post would get her attention.

"I really need a hair appointment," she said.

"I'll make the call now."

The only hair appointment I could get for my mother was at 9:30 a.m. on the day of the luncheon. The event started at 11:30 a.m., so our schedule would be tight. But it was doable.

AT 8:15 A.M. ON THE DAY of the literary luncheon, I went to my mother's bedroom, and knocked on the door.

"Mom, it's time to wake up."

"Give me fifteen," she said. As in, "Come back in fifteen minutes."

I rubbed my eyes, not in the mood for negotiating. I had a blistering headache, having consumed way too much wine the previous night—at home in a safe space, but clearly under the illusion that I was still in my twenties, and able to consume large quantities of alcohol without feeling hammer-headed the next morning.

"You're going to miss your hair appointment," I said, too loudly, my head throbbing. I had to curb my drinking. It was getting out of hand. But it was such a reliable way to blot out the demands of each day, keeping all those plates up in the air.

Why wasn't my mother responding? I clicked open her door.

"Mom, if you don't get up now we're going to be late."

"I'll get up in fifteen minutes," she insisted.

I loved her. I really did. But in that moment I wanted to grab her by the shoulders and shake her awake. The way she used to grab me as a child and say, "I'm going to shake some sense into you!" whenever I used profanity, jostling me hard—after first pouring pepper in my mouth to punish my brazen tongue.

Step away from the door, I told myself. *Take some Tylenol and pour yourself a cup of coffee.*

"Okay, I'll come back," I said. Calmly. Backing up.

I went downstairs, took two Extra Strength Tylenols and poured myself some coffee. Fifteen minutes later, I realized I hadn't heard any movement on the upstairs level. Irritated, I broke away from the breakfast table, climbed back upstairs, and opened my mother's door. She was still in bed.

"Come on, Mom," I said, about to lose my temper. But where would that get me?

My mother rolled over and looked at me like I was a total stranger.

"I made the appointment *for you*," I said, "not me."

The guilt tactic worked. My mother hauled herself up off the bed.

"I'm going to start calling you my compliance officer," she said, pouting.

"I don't care what you call me," I said. "As long as you comply."

Miraculously, within half-an-hour my mother managed to pull herself into an outfit that made her look better than I knew she felt. The wool skirt was a tight fit, but the pearls and cinnamon blush brought out her high cheekbones. Except for the hair, she looked fabulous. My mother even found time for a breakfast of cheese, toast, and jam. But then, as if lulled into overconfidence, she completely lost track of the time.

"Let's go," I said, swinging into the kitchen, buttoning up my winter coat. "Your hair appointment is in fifteen minutes."

My mother rounded the Formica counter with her dirty breakfast dishes. "I just have to brush my teeth and put on some lipstick," she said, sliding the dishes next to the sink. "I'll clean up later."

While my mother went up to her bedroom, I pulled out a black-and-white checked coat for her, and waited in the foyer. I checked my watch.

"What are you doing up there?" I said, from the bottom of the stairs.

"I'm coming!"

My mother descended the stairs, lit up with burgundy lips. I held up her coat, sleeves back.

"Not that one," she said. "The red cape matches my outfit better."

"Jesus," I said, huffing, hanging up the coat. The red cape it was.

WE ARRIVED AT THE Star Hair Salon at exactly 9:30 a.m. Inside the Dominican-style salon, the sound of sharp horns and a peppy rhythm filled the air. My mother's stylist approached us. She was long-haired, with almond eyes and fulsome cheeks. The kind that didn't need anti-aging products.

"Hello, Miss Helen," she said, giving my mother a hug. She stood back and fluffed my mother's hair as if rearranging flowers. She turned to me and said, "One-and-a-half hour."

I drove to the Flagship Carwash to indulge my LA-bred obsession with maintaining a clean car. The drive-through was cheaper than the hand wash, so I stayed in the convertible. As it lurched along the tracks, I thought uneasily about the hours ahead. The luncheon would probably be worthwhile—I might make a few business contacts—but I'd have to keep an eye on my mother, and make sure she didn't get lost in the crowd. Her moments of lucidity were still few and far between. I reminded myself that Tasha would be there to help keep tabs on her. Tasha was good with Mom. When she was around. I exhaled hard. I wished my sister was around more often.

Emerging from the other end of the carwash, I parked along the curb and got out to dry the stray wet spots on the car. I blotted the trunk, staring at the letters NOV in the upper left corner of the California license plate, and the yellow

2010 stamp on the upper right. I had renewed the tags just before my father died. According to the laws of Maryland, I had to switch out my plates within sixty days of taking up residence. I thought about fudging my arrival date to leave on my California plates as long as possible. I liked what they represented: a faded glory of sorts, and a hint of defiance.

By the time I got back to the house it was 10:15 a.m. I took a shower, slipped into a pair of black dress pants and a powder blue, fitted shirt, and added lipstick and pearl earrings. I felt like a changeling. I threw on a wool coat, hopped into my spotless car, and drove back to the hair salon.

Inside the salon, I saw my mother at the cashier counter, putting her Disney VISA card in her wallet. Her hair looked like a golden beach ball. She turned with a smile as I pulled up next to her.

"You look great," I said, amazed at the fact that my mother was eighty years old.

The only real giveaway was that she walked slowly, as if she were in leg irons. Just thinking about it made me sad. My mother's slow shuffle was the walk of the elderly. But she had never walked that way when my father was alive.

I gave her a kiss and intercepted the receipt my mother was about to put in her purse.

"Hold on a second," I said, scrutinizing the receipt.

My mother's shampoo and blowout cost fifty-five dollars. She had signed the receipt but left the tip line blank. "Did you give her cash?" I said in a low voice. "For the tip," I explained.

"Yes," said my mother.

"How much?"

"Five dollars."

"Five dollars?" I gasped.

My mother drew back, offended. "Well, that's not so bad."

"It's less than ten percent," I said, opening my wallet. "Mom, this isn't the Depression." She reached into her purse. "It's okay"—I stopped her—"I've got it."

I cut to her stylist and gave her an additional five dollars, then hustled my mother out of the salon, glancing at the wall clock. It was 11:15 a.m.

WE MADE IT TO THE literary luncheon more or less on time. I steered my mother into the crowded, chandeliered lobby of the Bethesda Country Club, set eyes on Tasha, and urged my mother in her direction. My sister came toward us, sizing up our mother. She gave me an approving look, like I'd pulled off an elaborate card trick.

"Take charge of her, would you?" I said, as an aside.

"Sure," Tasha said.

Her relaxed demeanor unnerved me. I was burned out and it wasn't even noon.

"You look beautiful," Tasha said to our mother, locking arms with her.

The three of us twisted through the lobby. Furtive glances at my mother turned to beaming smiles at me. Eyes betrayed concern. For me? My mother? Confused, I headed for a table stacked with books, and bought a copy of Pelecanos' novel *The Way Home*.

At the next table over, my mother produced her credit card and bought the George Tenet book, *At the Center of the*

Storm: My Years at the CIA. My mother's confidence level seemed to rise when she brought out her card. It was as if she were announcing to the world that despite her heartache she still had purchasing power.

"Should we go in?" said Tasha, bright-eyed.

I nodded, feeling overstimulated, and followed her and my mother into the massive banquet room. As we negotiated through the cloth-covered tables, a jumble of voices came at me from all directions. Everyone seemed to know everyone, backslapping and hugging in a collage of Brooks Brothers and St. John outfits. *So good to see you! Sit here! We're over there!*

"Aunt Lou wants you to sit with her," Tasha said to our mother. "I'll sit at the same table."

"I can sit anywhere," I said, happy to let my sister take over the Mom duties.

I heard one of the attendees ask my mother how she was doing.

"It's hard," was all my mother could get out.

I made a beeline for the far wall. The outer tables were always a safe bet in terms of finding an empty seat. At a table near the window, I collapsed into a chair and smiled at the thirty-something couple to my left. The guy thrust out a hand and said "Roger," nodding as our eyes met. We shook hands, and then he went back to scanning the room like a hunter on the savannah.

"And my name is Jill," said the woman next to him, her black hair pulled back into an efficient ponytail.

"Nice to meet you," I said. "Do you live nearby?"

"We live in DC," said Jill. "We just moved here from San Francisco."

"I used to live in LA," I said, surprised. "San Francisco is so different. In a good way."

"I miss it," said Jill. "But Roger got a great offer from his law firm, so—" she shrugged, "here we are! I work in marketing at IBM. What do you do?"

"Well... a few things," I said.

I felt trapped. What should I say? I knew I ran the house. I also knew that I looked after my mother. Actually it was more accurate to say that I was on call for her 24/7. But that wasn't a real job. Not the way Jill meant it.

I wracked my brain trying to think of how to describe my situation without using the words "in between jobs"—code for *casualty of the recession*. I didn't want to explain *why* I was in the predicament I was in, either, because that would involve mentioning my father's death, which I didn't want to talk about, mostly because the next question was always, "How's your mom doing?" which led to a discussion of how I spent much of my time coaxing her out of bed, or taking my mother to various appointments, and running errands for her. As opposed to working a *real job*.

My throat felt dry. When was this luncheon thing starting? I took a drink of water. Jill gave me an expectant look. I guess she was waiting for me elaborate on *what I do*.

"Mostly I sell anti-aging products," I blurted out, as if announcing I was a stripper. Like it was my dirty little secret. Which in a way it was, because I was such a reluctant seller.

"I need some of those," she said.

"Really?" I gave her face the once over. There weren't any obvious wrinkles, and her cheeks had a uniform coloration. But there was always room for improvement, and why waste a captive audience? Before long Jill gave me her business card and told me to call her the following week (I did but she was "in a meeting" that apparently never ended, because she never called back).

Finally, the emcee introduced the first author. I sat taller, searching for my mother, but I couldn't see her through the throng of guests. She was somewhere in the middle of the room. I hoped she was preparing to take notes for her article.

Among the four authors who spoke, the two Georges moved me the most. Pelecanos was memorable for his attire alone, looking dapper in a pinstriped suit and white, open-collar shirt. He spoke of how his father's endless hours of toil had bred a discipline by example, and about growing up with a sense of life's possibilities. It sounded so familiar. No matter what the job, I always worked hard at it, just like my father. And the sense of possibilities in life was right out of my mother's playbook. These were recurring themes in the Greek community, like genes passed down from generation to generation. I found the other George (Tenet) surprisingly self-effacing. I had recently seen him interviewed on *60 Minutes,* and thought he came across as unprepared and defensive. But here he seemed more relaxed, maybe because he was among fellow Greeks. He, too, spoke of his parents' humble roots and their deep impact on his life.

I was struck by the authors' unequivocal claims of owing everything to their parents in terms of setting the stage for their future success. Fame and fortune were incidental in light of the sacrifices that had been made on their behalf. I thought of all the adventures I'd had as a youth, made possible through my father's long hours of work, and all the time and energy my mother had put into organizing those adventures and helping me carry them out. She was a one-woman car service back then, driving me to piano, ballet, and violin lessons. And now the tables were turned: I was my mother's chauffeur, driving her to appointments, taking the wheel when we went out to dinner. *But that won't last*, I thought, convincing myself that our roles hadn't permanently reversed. My mother had recently said she wanted to start driving again, which meant my days of Driving Miss Helen were numbered.

I leaned sideways, trying again to get a look at my mother, but I just saw the backs of suit jackets and puffy heads of hair.

When the speeches ended, I headed into an anteroom where the authors were signing books. Ahead, I saw my mother entering the same room.

"There you are," I said, briefly concerned. My mother seemed unsure of what to do next, and whether she was in the right place. "Where's Tasha?"

"I don't know," said my mother.

"There's George Tenet." He was seated at a card table, pen in hand. "Why don't you have him sign your book?"

"Okay." My mother moved forward, lowering her head, like she didn't want to be noticed.

I went to Pelecanos' table. He seemed alternately amused and uncomfortable by all the attention he was getting. "Is that right?" he said, grinning modestly when I told him how his letters had fueled my writing. He didn't seem to remember me, but I didn't care. I felt uplifted, as if my life had come full circle, the past now present.

I soaked up the lively scene, unexpectedly strengthened by my larger Greek family, eager to get back to work on the Greek food and culture show. By now Callie and I had sketched out a few story lines and chosen a name for the show: *Ouzo, Olives, Opa!* And I had started drafting the treatment—a narrative description of the show.

Driving home from the luncheon, I felt all fired up.

"Did you have a good time?" I asked my mother.

"Yes," she said. "It was nice."

A silence fell between us, one of those alone-together silences I was still getting used to.

"I saw you talking with George Tenet," I said.

"They came to your dad's funeral," said my mother.

All roads led back to my father. "Did he inscribe your book?"

"Yes."

When we arrived back at the house, my mother deposited her purse and nylon gift bag at the base of the foyer stairs and then went into the family room. I opened her gift bag, curious to see how Tenet had inscribed her copy of *At the Center of the Storm*. But the first pages were blank. Had my mother accidentally brought home someone else's copy? Or had she remembered incorrectly?

Entering the family room, I saw my mother's stocking feet propped up on one end of the short leather couch. She had wasted no time in assuming her preferred horizontal position. I went into the kitchen to check the phone for messages, vexed by the dirty breakfast dishes sitting out on the kitchen counter. The toaster was out—normally it was tucked away in a cupboard—pools of butter were splashed on the cutting board built into the countertop, and there were crumbs everywhere. The idea of cleaning the place up crossed my mind, but then

I thought, *I'm not the maid.* And I had work to do upstairs. There weren't any phone messages.

I wheeled out of the kitchen. "Don't forget about the dishes, please."

"I won't," said a disembodied voice from the other side of the couch.

I sped upstairs and changed into a pair of jeans and wool turtleneck, on a high from the luncheon. Over the next couple of hours, I revised the treatment for *Ouzo, Olives, Opa!* and drafted a logline for the program, boiling it down to a two-line description I could live with.

It was dark outside by the time I went to get a can of seltzer from the kitchen. When I saw the dirty dishes on the counter, I stopped midstride. Dismayed, I went into the family room and found my mother exactly where I'd left her: flat on her back, with her eyes shut, and her arms at her sides like a mummy.

"Mom, you said you were going to clean up the kitchen."

"I'm going to," she said.

"When?"

"Later," she replied, turning her head sideways.

"It's almost dinner time." I paused, impatient. "What's going on?"

"What do you mean?"

"Will you please tell me why you haven't cleaned up in the kitchen? Your dirty dishes have been sitting there for eight hours."

"I… I kept thinking about your dad at the luncheon," my mother said. "He should have been there with me." She put a hand on her forehead. "I looked at all the other husbands there, and I imagined your dad on my arm, or getting me a glass of wine from the bar like he always did." She wiped her eyes. "It was awful."

I felt terrible for my mother, but I was almost hyperventilating. I had no idea the luncheon had affected her that way, and it took her so long to tell me. I handed her a tissue, sat on the arm of the couch, and let out a deep breath.

"Mom, you have to tell me what you're feeling," I said. "How could I possibly know how hard that was for you?" I kept thinking, *I'm not trained for this. How is this supposed to work?*

I had not foreseen the significance of the luncheon, but now it seemed obvious. It was my mother's first solo outing since my father's death, and she wasn't ready to be seen at a social function, least of all one where there would be so many people she and my father had known from their decades of living in the DC area.

I tried to put myself in her position. But how could I? I wasn't married for fifty-six years, used to having everyone see me as part of a twosome. Did my mother feel that her friends at the luncheon were staring at her in pity? Or avoiding her altogether, like a contagious disease?

I remembered the weight of social status in my hometown. The subtle ranking and filing that went on at every high profile event. Low profile events, too. I found it dull and detestable. But my mother had been immersed in this status game for ages, moving confidently through the scene with my father at her side. And now she was without him. I realized her status had changed. She was no longer Mrs. Peter E. Panarites. Now she was Helen P. Panarites. Single, like me.

I left the family room, frazzled. But at least my mother and I had aired our thoughts. And she had promised to get up in five minutes and attend to those dirty dishes.

An hour later, I came back downstairs and saw she was no longer in the family room. When I went into the kitchen and saw it was still in a state of disarray, I felt like I'd been sucker-punched. Zombie-like, I began rinsing the dirty dishes and transferring them to the dishwasher. I put away the toaster and sponged down the counter. These were such small chores, but doing them felt like moving a barrel full of bricks.

Afterward I discovered my mother in her bedroom, flat on her back, on top of the bed sheets, eyes closed. I entered as if sleepwalking.

"Mom," I said.

"What is it now?"

Where had that cold-blooded voice come from? I just wanted to say my piece and leave.

"The thing is... running the house is a lot of work. I can't do it alone. If you say you're going to clean up after yourself, you have to actually do it."

"I'll get to it eventually." My mother sat up, as if it were now pointless to try and get any shuteye. "I don't go at your speed."

"I'm not asking you to go at my speed," I said.

Her eyes cut into mine. "Then why are you giving me such a hard time?"

I felt the blood rush to my face. "Mom, this isn't a competition. I'm asking for your help." My legs gave way, and I fell to my knees. "This house is huge. I can't do everything."

"Oh, for heaven's sakes," she said. "Don't be so dramatic." She took a tissue from the night table, and unceremoniously blew her nose.

I pushed off the carpet and moved toward the door. "You know what?" I said, lips quivering. "You're not the only one who misses Dad."

I went into my father's den, closed the door, and called my sister Tasha. By the time she answered the phone I was crying uncontrollably. I hadn't cried like that since my father died.

"*Mom* said that?" Tasha gasped, after I spat out the story.

"Yes." I took a breath. "The sleeping I understand. The lack of conversation—I get it, she's grieving, and in shock. But lashing out at me? I don't even know who that person is."

I literally did not recognize my mother. I knew she was strong-willed, but it wasn't in her nature to be combative, never mind downright nasty. In fact the only change I had seen in her behavior since my father's death was her withdrawing from life.

"I don't know how to handle this," I sobbed. "What do I do?"

"You guys need an intervention," said Tasha. "Hang up the phone. When I call back let Mom answer then pick up."

I followed my sister's instructions, glad for her help, but thrown by her clinical approach. The phone rang five times before I heard my mother say "hello?" from her bedroom. I picked up the corded phone in the den. In a sunny voice Tasha asked my mother if she'd started organizing her luncheon notes for the *Herald* article. My mother said she hadn't taken any notes, and planned to write the entire piece from memory.

"Oh—okay," said Tasha, as if wondering how that would work. "So, what are you up to now?"

"Same old," my mother sighed. "You know, just getting through the day."

I expected her next phrase would be *that sister of yours is a real pain in the ass.*

"I know it isn't easy," said Tasha.

I marveled at her coolheaded approach. Then I remembered she wasn't here getting emotionally banged up or desperate to earn a living.

My mother let out a heavy sigh. That was encouraging, a sign that her veil of indifference had been pierced. After confirming that I was on the line, Tasha brought up my Mayday call. She replayed the facts of our conversation.

"Maybe we should all go back to grief counseling," Tasha said.

Yes, I thought. *We should all go together.* If Tasha came with us, I would feel less alone.

"I'll go along with whatever you girls decide," said my mother, resigned.

I felt some of the tension leave my body. Her willingness to *go along with whatever you girls decide* meant my mother could accept a hard truth when I wasn't the only one laying it at her feet. That was the advantage of getting Tasha involved in our spat. Yet it seemed unlikely we would have had the fight at all if Tasha or Zoë were around, because one of them would have stepped in to clean up the mess in the kitchen.

I hung up the phone, relieved, but also worried; what if the next disagreement with my mother involved a face-off like this one? What if all our disagreements played out like this?

One of us had to change. I knew it would have to be me, because my mother was too wrapped up in her grief to consider anyone's needs but her own. That was my own hard truth. I decided that, from now on, I would just give in to my mother's sloppy ways and avoid taking them personally. I would learn to live with her messes, or clean up if they got on my nerves. Fighting wasn't an option. I had to conserve my energy. I had to save myself.

I went into my mother's bedroom and sat next to her. She was slumped over, as if she'd just been pulled out of a burning building. I put an arm around her.

"It won't always be this hard," I said, unsure whether I believed my own words.

SHORTLY BEFORE OUR PLANNED grief-counseling session, I got a call from Tasha.

"I'm really sorry," she said, "but I can't make it today."

"Why?" I said, incredulous.

"I have a conference call I can't get out of."

"During lunch?" I knew things came up, but this grief-counseling session was critical.

"The call starts at eleven," said Tasha. "I won't be able to get to you in time. I'm sorry."

"Right. I've got to go."

I hung up, telling myself to just get in the car and go to the session. Which I did, filled with despair, convincing myself that returning to Montgomery Hospice would be beneficial for at least two members of our family. In fact, the fallout from the literary luncheon suggested our session with Awa would be more like couples counseling than grief counseling.

Clearly, my mother and I were now on our own, and we had some work to do where avoiding scrapes was concerned.

When we arrived at Montgomery Hospice, the grief counselor Awa greeted us warmly in the lobby. She led us once again to the Victorian parlor cave. I settled into the familiar velvet loveseat, and my mother resumed her position in the brocaded chair.

"I've never seen my mother so sad," I said, starting the session. I didn't want to rehash our argument over the dirty dishes. My mother knew what prompted our visit, and Awa didn't need specifics. "I wish there was something I could do, but I feel powerless. And it's affecting our living situation."

"Helen?" said Awa, looking at my mother with hopeful, encouraging eyes.

"Peter and I took so many trips together," my mother said. "Italy, Spain, Dubrovnik…."

I guess it didn't occur to her to address anything I'd said, because from there my mother continued reminiscing about her life with Dad, repeating phrases from our last session with Awa. I felt as if I were in a recurring dream from which I would never escape. But at least I had the chance to lay bare my frustrations, in a neutral place, away from our haunted house. That was enough, then.

8
Go-To Girl

Four months since Dad's death.

Spring was on the horizon, but the weather hadn't turned. The days were still biting cold in Maryland, and the skies perennially gray, like a hangover that won't quit. A dose of tropical sunshine was in order. For my mother, not me. I suggested she escape the wintry weather and visit Zoë in West Palm Beach.

By now my mother had become a bit more sociable, allowing herself to be picked up for the occasional lunch date or accept the overture of friends who wanted to stop by for a visit.

"Come down and say hello to Sherry," my mother said, when her former White House colleague dropped in for tea.

Sherry was pleasant enough, but stopping to *say hello* meant being yanked out of my intoxicating work rhythm.

At the same time, I didn't want to seem rude, so I popped downstairs, spent a few minutes with the effervescent Sherry, and then excused myself.

Ditto with my mother's friend, Ginny, who spoke so fast and at such length that it was all I could do to cut in with: "Excuse me, but I have to get back to work."

"Will you come with me?" said my mother, when I suggested the trip to Florida.

"I'd like to," I said, craving a vacation. "But I have to keep working on the Greek show."

By now I had thrown in the towel with my anti-aging business and abandoned the work entirely. There had been no need for a formal resignation; the way the business worked, the end of my recruitment efforts simply meant the end of potential commissions. Callie and I were in high gear on *Ouzo, Olives, Opa!,* having traded dozens of e-mails and phone calls, and spent long hours at each other's homes developing the written pitch package. All the while we fed off each other's goofy energy, giggling our way through the invention of plot lines and jokes we thought every immigrant family could relate to. The experience was uplifting, and kept my sorrow at bay, both for my father's death and the heartache I felt for my mother.

"We'll probably have to shoot a sizzle reel," I told Callie, at our latest rendezvous. I paused at her vacant look. I forgot that she had never worked in television production. "A short video," I added. "To give people we're pitching the show to a sense of its style and elements."

"I don't have a video camera," Callie said.

"Tasha has one we can borrow. It's nothing fancy, but it's free."

"We can film at the Greek festival. It's at the end of April."

"Perfect." I was already working out a shot list in my head.

Tasha's neighbor, a senior development executive at Discovery Studios, was available to meet with us in early April. I was thrilled at the opportunity to meet with such a high-ranking executive. After months of flailing about, it seemed my professional life was slowly coming together.

But I kept getting distracted by my duties on the home front, and when calamity struck, I realized how precarious the balance of my life was.

By now I had signed my mother up for twice-weekly physical therapy sessions to address the pain in her back. The therapist was an Israeli woman with sparkling eyes and the body of a Sumo wrestler. She did not tolerate tardiness, as I learned when we arrived ten minutes late to my mother's first PT session.

"You absolutely must be on time," she said, wagging a finger at me. "Otherwise we cancel the session. Because there are people behind you, and then the whole schedule is off."

"Sorry," I said, red-faced. "Usually I *am* on time."

This was true when I was on my own, but getting my mother into the car was an X-factor I couldn't control. Having to herd her into the car at all was foreign, after my freewheeling, solo life in LA.

"We'll be on time for Friday's appointment," I assured the physical therapist.

On that Friday morning, while my mother was preparing to leave the house—brushing her teeth and putting on her lipstick—I went downstairs to get the car started. As usual we were cutting it close time-wise, so I was already feeling cranky.

The entrance to the garage was just beyond the laundry room in the basement of our house. Nearing the room, I smelled something rancid and poked my head inside, halting in my tracks. The double-basin sink was filled to the brim with water. Bits of lettuce were floating on the surface, mixed in with carrot peelings and decomposed tomatoes.

I snatched up a dishwashing tub and began bailing out the basin, carting water outdoors in a run/walk fever. After four bails, I ran upstairs, pulse racing.

"Mom—we have to leave now!" I called out to her.

She came out of her bedroom putting on her earrings. "I'm coming," she said. "I'll be down in five minutes."

"You said that twenty minutes ago!"

I ran into the kitchen, directly above the laundry room, and studied the water that had risen halfway up the sink. I flipped on the wall switch. The water in the sink bubbled up like molten lava. I cut the disposal, shot to the phone, and called our neighbor Betty.

"Oh, hi Jana!" she said, bouncy as usual. "How's your mom doing? I've been meaning to call, but we've just been so busy with these grandkids and—"

"Sorry—" I cut her off—"but I'm in a rush. Our kitchen sink is backed up. I was wondering if you could give me the name of a plumber." I fumbled for a pen and paper.

"Oh, sure. We use James Wheat & Sons. They're terrific. I'll get the number for you."

"Great." I began pacing the floor. Biting my thumbnails. Waiting. *Shit, we're going to be late again!* I thought. I could already see the physical therapist shaming me with a wag of the finger. And where was my mother? I covered the phone.

"Mom! Are you coming down?" No answer.

Betty came back on the line and I scribbled down the number. "Thanks so much."

I called the plumber. "It's an emergency," I said. "Can you send someone today?" They had an opening in the afternoon.

"I'll be here." I gave the lady the address, hung up, and rushed toward the basement, to make sure the water in the laundry room hadn't risen. At the bottom of the stairs, I saw my mother descending the last steps. That was when I lost it.

"I don't know why you say you'll be ready in five minutes," I snapped, "when you really mean half an hour."

The problem was I believed my mother when she said she would be ready in five minutes. I kept thinking she was the old punctual Mom, not the new Mom with no concept of time.

"Your dad knew all my foibles," she said, starting to cry.

"Well, I'm not Dad. And you lived together for fifty-six years so he had a long time to learn those foibles, and a big incentive to do so because you were both doing things for each other. But now I'm doing everything for both of us. And we're late, and the laundry room sink is backed up, and I have to deal with that when we get back at the same time as I'll be trying to work with Callie."

"Okay, okay," said my mother.

Like I was being unreasonable. But of course I sounded like a shrew.

We arrived late to the physical therapy appointment, but not as late as the last time. And fate was on my side: the therapist was behind schedule. She apologized to me!

At least flare-ups like this between my mother and me didn't happen too often, because I'd gotten better at faking her out, telling her we had to leave the house sooner than we actually did. As with mounting a dry-eraser board on the wall for scheduling purposes, I was always fine-tuning the system. But when disaster struck my anxiety soared, and I wanted to go into a corner and cry. I always resisted the urge. I literally couldn't spare the time.

All the more reason to send my mother off to Florida. I craved some breathing room, a window of appointment-free days when I was responsible only for myself.

"Why don't you go to Florida with Thea?" I said to my mother. "Zoë is up for it."

"I don't know," said my mother. "I've never gotten on a plane without your dad."

"Mom, sooner or later you'll have to make that leap," I said. "If you want to go on living. Which I hope you do."

"I don't have a choice," said my mother.

"Of course you do. Everyone has a choice. You can choose to embrace life or throw it away." I faltered. "I know it's not easy, but—well, the way you say that just makes me so sad. Because you're in good health for the most part. And a lot of women your age are active."

My mother lowered her head. "I just can't imagine flying without your dad."

"I'll help you," I said. "I'll put you on the plane myself."

"But if I go to Florida, you'll be all alone in the house. Won't you get lonely?"

"Nope."

My mother gave me a wry look. "You need a break from me, don't you?"

"Kind of," I said.

Not to say our relationship was always a bed of nails, but I was worried about my mother's growing dependence on me. I thought it would lessen over time, but it only seemed to be getting worse. I was her go-to girl for everything.

"Jana!" she called out to me one day from the foyer. "When you have a moment, can you come down here and help me with something?"

"What do you need, Mom?" I yelled, bothered that she'd broken my concentration. I was at my desk, in the throes of fine-tuning the synopsis for the pilot episode of the Greek show.

"I can't get this damned computer to work," she said.

I guessed she was drafting her article about the literary luncheon for the *Herald*. This was definitely worth getting up for. It was the first time since my father's death that my mother had resumed one of her past joys. I dashed to the basement, where my mother kept her office. Her computer and wall of files were opposite the furnace, and adjacent to the washing machine and dryer. Several years ago I asked my mother if it bothered her to work in such an austere atmosphere. She surprised me by saying "not at all," explaining that it was the only place in the house where no one would bother her and she could disappear into her own world. Her blunt assessment was a refreshing (and rare) acknowledgment that she had an identity apart from my father.

"What have you got here?" I said, parking myself in front of her computer, staring uncertainly at the ten lines on the screen with my mother's name at the bottom.

"It's my article for the *Herald*," she said. "I can't figure out how to save the document."

"Is this the whole thing?"

"Yes."

"It's… not very long," I said.

"Oh?"

"Mom, that's not an article," I said, heavyhearted. "It's more like an announcement."

She looked down. "But it's a good start," I added quickly.

How could my mother think that was an article? There was hardly anything on the page. And the words didn't quite fit together:

> *They all identified their zeal for writing with their Greek roots. The occasion marked their contribution to their ethnicity. Pelacanos is particularly known for his crime fiction, and was nominated for the Best Dramatic Series at the February 2010 ceremony for his work on The Wire for the show's fifth and final season "Late Editions." The receptive audience wanted to be connected to this well known literary writer and expressed their admiration for being representative of the Greek mind.*

Was something wrong with my mother's brain? I was worried, but wanted to keep her going in a positive direction. I retrieved a foldout chair from the utility room.

"Why don't you sit down next to me," I said, "and we'll write it together."

"Are you sure?" said my mother. "I don't want to use up your time."

"It's okay," I said. "I want to help you."

But I didn't realize how long it would take. Besides investing a few hours on the writing, I had to track down a photograph of the four authors who'd spoken, to accompany the story. And I wound up writing most of the article, drawing on my own memories rather than my mother's, because she couldn't seem to recall anything about the event. On paper and out loud, the only language my mother seemed fluent in was the language of Peter; her memories of my father came out in a flawless patter, but every other topic produced a mishmash of thoughts and words.

My heart beat faster, thinking about my mother's foggy brain. But maybe it was due entirely to her grief. I told myself I should wait a little longer before subjecting her to any cognitive testing. *And that will be all on you,* I realized, stiffening. Because who else had the flexibility in her schedule to take my mother to the appointment? Who else was even around to detect the changes in her behavior? My sisters heard about them secondhand—from me, not our mother. She put on a brave face when speaking with my sisters, as if her suffering shouldn't seep beyond the walls of our house. It was up to me to paint the true picture, which I did in countless e-mails to my sisters, craving the comfort of a shared experience even if I was shouldering the burden.

I focused on the positive because that was my instinct. I told myself that at least my mother had *tried* to write the article. Maybe she'd lost her mind, but she hadn't lost her will.

IN THE END my mother agreed to go to Florida with her sister for a little more than two weeks. I counted it as a win-win for both of us. The day before she left, I remembered I needed to organize her pills and tuck them in her luggage. She could forget to pack a girdle or a bra, but I couldn't allow her to forget those medications. Such was my life that I reflexively backed up my mother, always thinking for both of us, like a pregnant woman eating for two.

I stopped working, pushing away from my desk to organize my mother's pills. I moved into the hallway and headed to my mother's bedroom. Halfway there, I felt my legs slowing, as if I'd encountered a UFO. The door to my father's bathroom was wide open. I couldn't believe it. After all these months, I had missed the unveiling. When did my mother open the door? Why didn't she tell me? Did she want the experience to be private? Standing in the opened door, I faced the site of my father's collapse. *She did it*, I thought. A demon had been slayed.

MY MOTHER WAS RIGHT: I did get a little lonely without her around. After she left for Florida, the house felt cavernous. But it was blissfully conducive to writing, and working without any interruptions was a vacation of its own.

I slept late, lazed around the house, and met up with a few friends from grad school who were now living in DC. They were all nearly half my age, working tirelessly for little money at meaningful day jobs like organizing student exchange programs and advancing the cause of civil rights. I felt lucky to have them nearby. They made me laugh, and I felt less isolated knowing we could meet for dinner or drinks when I needed a break from the comatose suburbs.

But I could go only so long without thinking about my mother. I didn't miss her so much as stew about whether she was safe, which was ridiculous, because I knew my mother was in safe hands. Zoë had intercepted her and my aunt at the

US Airways gate the minute their plane had landed. She had cooked for the ladies, gone shopping with them, and included them in plans with friends. So why was I obsessing? I realized I'd become a helicopter parent with my mother.

And then one day while I was pecking away at my laptop, I began daydreaming about the Florida sunshine. Tired of the winter, I imagined my mother lounging by the pool under a palm tree, asleep under the baking sun or deep in a nonfiction book. *Should I call her?* I thought, aware that part of me was looking for an excuse to stop working. I closed out of my document and called Mom on her cell phone.

"Heh—hello?" she said.

"Hi Mom." It sounded like she was having trouble breathing. "What are you doing?"

"I'm going to get my hair done," she said, sucking in air.

"Oh." I paused, puzzled. "Are you walking to the salon?"

"Yes," she said. "And I've been at it for quite a while."

I felt a rush of adrenaline. The image of my octogenarian mother lazing by the pool morphed into one of her staggering up the sidewalk with beads of sweat gathering on her face.

"You don't sound so good," I said. "Are you okay?"

"Uh… I can't seem to find the salon," said my mother.

"Are you walking north or south? I mean—" What was I thinking? My mother wouldn't know which direction she was walking. But I knew the area well, having visited Zoë often.

"What stores are you near?" I said.

"I don't see any names," said my mother.

"Can you see any street signs?"

The line went silent. Was my mother dehydrated? About to collapse? I told myself to calm down and speak slowly.

"Mom, are you on the residential road with palm trees, or the four-lane road with shops?"

"The road with shops," she wheezed.

"Okay. Find a shady spot, and please stay there," I said. "I'm going to call Zoë, and call you right back."

I phoned Zoë and told her our mother was lost on Dixie Highway. In a matter of seconds I explained where I thought she was located.

"Jesus," Zoë said. "She's way off base."

"Welcome to my world." I paused to get hold of my emotions. "Zoë, no matter what Mom says, you can't take it for granted that she knows where she's going."

"I'm leaving now," she said.

I called my mother and told her Zoë was on her way. Fortunately her office was close by.

It turned out my mother had overshot her destination by nearly two miles. I thought, *what if I hadn't called?* A list of potential outcomes flooded my mind, none of them good.

The incident sealed my fate. I realized my mother was my ward, and I was her guardian. I knew that as long as she was alive, I would never be able to relax.

9

Drowning, Not Waving

Five months since Dad's death.

By now I had fallen into a pattern of living where putting out fires was the norm. I was in reactive mode. No landline, television or Internet service? That FIOS bundle was the lifeblood of our house. A quick check of the router revealed the lights that usually blinked were now black. In a flash I called Verizon, ordered a new router, and set it up. A few days later I stepped into a pool of water on the main floor. The ceiling was dripping wet. I scrambled to find a contractor who came by and patched it up. Tree limbs littered the driveway after countless thunderstorms; a call to the landscaper and it was all hauled away. The power cut out, the heater malfunctioned, and light bulbs seemed to burn out daily. And then there was that water-filled basin in the laundry room.

"The disposal is pretty much shot," said the plumber, peering down the kitchen sink. "Do you know how old it is?"

"No idea," I said.

"Well, that was the cause of your backup," he said.

I watched him gather up the tarp spread across the floor, thinking, *this can't happen again.*

"How much would a new disposal cost?"

"I'd have to check," said the plumber. "But I can send you a quote for an InSinkErator. It's professional grade. Not readily available to the public."

Later that day I received his quote: $801 including installation. Aghast, I researched the InSinkErator online, and found it was *readily available* at a nearby plumbing store for $250. Installed at $200 (by a new plumber), the total cost came to $450. I felt giddy at the savings.

But I couldn't afford to get complacent. Braced for malfunction always, I pushed through the endless repairs, fitting them into my tight schedule. If I was falling apart I didn't know it; I was too caught up in holding everything together, unable to imagine any other way of living.

"You should get a physical," said Tasha, calling me on her way home from work one day.

"I feel fine," I said, brushing it off. "Besides, I don't have time."

"It won't take that long."

"But I don't have health insurance."

"Mom will pay for it," said Tasha.

Recoiling, I thought, *she's not a multimillionaire.* And so what if I was running myself ragged? It wasn't like I was having regular chest pains.

"A check-up can't be that expensive," Tasha said. "Call Dr. Brosnan. She's my doctor. You'll love her. She's younger than Mom's doctor, and works in the same building."

My first thought was: I could check off two boxes at once, see Dr. Brosnan on a day when Mom had an appointment with Dr. Post. If there was a way to save time, I'd find it.

"Are you exercising?" my sister Zoë asked the next day, getting in on the act.

"Yes," I said. "I go for a walk every morning."

"That's good… because you're carrying the load, as the primary caregiver."

Caregiver? I thought, stumped. *Is that what I am now?* I knew I looked after my mother, but this sounded like a professional designation. I wasn't a nurse, was I? Or was a caregiver something different? Believe it or not, I had never even heard the term.

"I am healthy," I said, thinking, *and I won't always be a caregiver—or whatever you want to call me.* I bristled at the thought of being labeled in any way.

"I'm just saying, you sound tense every time I talk to you," said Zoë. "You have to be careful not to overexert yourself."

Easy for you to say. I knew my sister meant well, but I didn't know how anyone in my position could avoid overexertion. But both of my sisters had raised the issue, independently of each other, so maybe they were onto something. I thought I might as well get it over with.

"Hi—yes," I said, calling the medical office. "I'd like to make an appointment for a physical exam with Dr. Brosnan."

"She isn't taking any new patients," said her assistant.

Slap. "Uh… could she possibly make an exception? My sister is one of her regular patients."

"Hold the line, please."

Classical music blasted in my ear. I jerked away from the phone, scanning the dry eraser calendar on the wall, where the month of April was mapped out.

"Ma'am," the assistant clicked in. "Dr. Brosnan has an opening on June twenty-first. Can you come in at 10:15 a.m.?"

June seemed like an eternity to wait. On the other hand, it bought me some time.

"I'll check." I flipped to June in my monthly planner. My eyes lit up. My mother had an appointment with Dr. Post on June 21, at 10:00 a.m. "I'll be there," I said.

THE NEXT DAY I flung open the door at Starbucks, my stomach fluttering with nervousness. I set eyes on my writing partner Callie, chatting with a woman I took to be Wendy, the executive at Discovery. She was right out of an L.L. Bean catalogue, with a quilted vest and windswept bob.

"Can I get you something to drink?" I said, arriving at the table, playing hostess.

"A cappuccino would be great," said Wendy.

"Callie?"

"I'm good," she said.

I whipped to the counter, inhaling the bitter aroma of coffee as I ordered from the barista. Back at the table, I delivered the goods, and sat down.

"Thanks," said Wendy. "So, tell me about your show."

"It's a cross between *My Life on the D-List* and *Anthony Bourdain's 'No Reservations,'* I said. "We're calling it *Ouzo, Olives, Opa!*—with Callie as the host."

"Or tour guide," said Callie. "Through the colorful world of Greek food and culture."

"The format of the show will vary slightly from week to week," I said, "but it will be an hour long, so viewers can get to know the cast of characters. And in every episode, Callie will be confronted by some Greek food challenge."

"For instance, in the first episode," said Callie, "I freak out when I hear my *dolmathes*—those are stuffed grape leaves—are expected to be the hit at an upcoming, international potluck dinner. Since I'm Greek, my friends just assume I have the best recipe. But I've never made *dolmathes* from scratch, and, of course, those are the best. So I get a lesson from the *real* experts: the church ladies who are busy preparing food for the upcoming Greek festival."

"We're going to film that for the sizzle reel," I said.

"Excellent," said Wendy.

"At the end of every episode," I said, "viewers will be left with a workable recipe they can try at home, along with some common-sense approaches to life, handed down through the ages."

"Well," said Wendy, "as far as pitching it at Discovery, there are lots of different networks, and they each have their own brand and targeted audience."

"What about TLC?" I said, referring to The Learning Channel. "It's an educational show as much as a food show."

"I'm not sure what they're doing right now," said Wendy. "But I'll find out for you."

"Should we be pitching to any particular production company in town?" I felt a little insecure about being an unknown quantity in DC, but I knew I had the chops to be a producer, and I didn't mind being one of many, as was often the case with television shows. I viewed the Greek show in terms of laying the groundwork for future projects. Uppermost on my mind was drawing a salary of some kind, in order to eventually move out of the house.

"There's Reed Street Productions," said Wendy. "And Pop Media—I've worked with the owners. They're ethical, and seasoned. Try pitching them first, and come back to me if they pass."

"We'll do that," I said. "Thank you."

After we said our goodbyes, I sat for a moment, my head spinning with next steps.

"We're going to have a show on TV!" said Callie, squealing. "I can't wait to tell my friends!"

"I wouldn't." I didn't mean to sound like a killjoy, but creative success had never come easily in my life and we still had to produce the sizzle reel. That would involve extensive filming and editing by a professional editor, because it couldn't look shoddy. The reel would be our main selling tool.

"I need to research those production companies," I said, heading toward the exit with Callie on my heels.

"And I'll find out when the food prep starts for the Greek festival," said Callie. "I think it's next weekend."

"Get ready to be on camera."

"Oh, I'm ready," said Callie.

BACK AT HOME, I googled the two production companies Wendy had mentioned in our meeting. It turned out the founders of Pop Media had previously worked at Discovery. Several of their current programs were now airing on the Discovery networks. Reed Street Productions was the only other local company actively producing nonfiction television programs for the major networks. Being a global media company, Discovery was the third and by far the biggest player.

I felt uneasy. It seemed we *had* to hitch our wagons to one of these three production companies, or we wouldn't get anywhere with our show in DC. I had a friend in New York who might be able to hook us up with a company there, but New York was the nearest major production hub. We were too far from LA, where we could have pitched our show all over town.

It only takes one, I thought, refusing to set myself up for defeat by focusing on the limitations of where I lived. I reminded myself that we had a strong ally in Wendy. In fact I had only been home for a few hours when I noticed she had taken action on our behalf. She forwarded me an e-mail from the Director of Development at Pop Media, who wrote: "We would love to meet and learn more about your project." But the head of development asked that I first sign and return her attached Standard Submission Agreement.

A FLURRY OF E-MAIL communications followed. I began fielding them the next day, before, during, and after my mother's appointment with her eye doctor. Apparently she hadn't had an exam for two years. The only reason I knew this was because when we were at the Department of Motor Vehicles renewing her driver's license, my mother failed her vision test.

"I guess we have to come back," my mother said, defeated, as we moved away from the cubicle at the DMV.

"Yup," I said, distressed, thinking, *wonder where I'll fit that into my schedule?* But my mother needed to start driving again and she couldn't do it without that new license.

"I'll call your eye doctor and make the appointment now. What's his name?"

"Dr. Hargrove," said my mother. "He's in Bethesda."

While we were at the DMV, I sadly relinquished my California driver's license, exchanging it for one from the state of Maryland. And I purchased new license plates, promptly throwing them in the trunk of my car, refusing to give up my California plates yet.

Now we were riding up the elevator to my mother's eye appointment.

Entering the doctor's office, I was jolted by the dated waiting room—taupe everywhere, dimly lit, filled with fake plants and old ophthalmology equipment set out like museum pieces. I made vacant eye contact with a diminutive blonde behind the counter, wearing the nametag: Grace. She gave me a passing glance before beaming at my mother in surprise.

"Hi!" she said. "How are you?"

"Not so well," said my mother. "My husband died."

Stone cold shock. "Oh my gosh," said Grace. "When did that happen? I'm *so* sorry."

"Last year," said my mother. "Two days before Thanksgiving."

A wave of sorrow seemed to roll through the air, like tear gas.

"Why don't we sit down," I said, seeing my BlackBerry flashing red at the corner.

A technician in a white coat came out of a back room. "Helen Panarites?"

"Here we are," I said with an urgent wave.

My mother did a one-eighty, following the technician into the examining room. Grace tracked her, wide-eyed, like she was witnessing a live birth.

"Are you her daughter?" she said in a cheery voice.

I was about to sit down, but stopped. "Yes."

"It's so good of you to bring her in," said Grace. "Gosh, it must be awful for her."

Why was she looking at me so intensely? I wanted to sit, but I felt like my feet wouldn't move.

"Do you live here?" said Grace.

"Yes... I"—my eyes flitted to the flashing red corner of my phone—"I just moved here, from California. Actually, I'm living with Mom."

"Oh, that's wonderful!" said Grace. "Are you staying?"

"For the time being," I said.

"Your mom really needs you," said Grace. She wrinkled her nose. "How did he die?"

I almost fell over. All these months after my father's death, I still wasn't used to the question, but it kept coming up, usually when I was with my mother. No one dared ask her, but they felt free to ask me.

"He had a heart attack," I said, thoughts scattered. "He just... collapsed."

Grace's hand went to her mouth. "Oh gosh," she said.

"Excuse me, I have to—" I held up my BlackBerry.

"Oh yes, I'm sorry," said Grace.

I sat on the oatmeal couch, trying to rid myself of the image of my father crumpled up on the bathroom floor. I glanced at my phone and began punching out an e-mail to my friend Greg in LA: "At eye appt w mom… This is what I called about (assuming u get attachmt)." I forwarded him the Standard Submission Agreement from Pop Media. Greg was an entertainment lawyer. I wanted him to review the language in the agreement before I signed it.

After that I scrolled through my e-mails and flipped through an old issue of National Geographic, restless. Thirty minutes later my mother appeared in the lobby, eyes squelched together, postdilation.

"I need a new prescription," she said, handing me a piece of paper, smiling dreamily as if coming off a morphine drip.

"Colonial Opticians is right around the corner," said Grace.

"Could we go there now?" my mother asked.

"Uh…" I hesitated, eager to get home and reread the submission agreement. But I knew my mother couldn't retake her DMV vision test without a new pair of eyeglasses. And I thought getting them now would boost her spirits. "Okay," I said. "Let's do it."

Off to the optician's we went. Slowly, of course, with our arms interlocked. I yearned to move faster, but willed myself to be patient, thinking, *you can teach yourself to slow down.* It was such a new experience. I felt like I was learning how to crawl.

ONCE WE GOT BACK to the house, I located the two-page submission agreement I'd printed out from Pop Media, and read the document in a state of disbelief. The company wanted us to waive a bunch of rights to our material, and agree to let them sell our material to anyone without telling us or paying us. I couldn't fathom why Wendy thought the owners of this company were ethical. They didn't even know what we had, and they were already asking us to hand it over, basically for free.

I slumped in my chair, conflicted. I wanted to pitch our project, but the way the agreement was worded, we would be left with no leverage. The agreement needed to be revised, to be fairer to all parties. I sent an e-mail to the company, requesting some changes, but Pop Media wouldn't budge. And they wouldn't meet with us unless we signed their submission agreement first. In the end, we declined; there were too many Catch-22s.

I felt dizzy from all the back-and-forth e-mails, and dejected by the outcome. But there were other avenues to pursue, and I wasn't giving up on my treasured show. By now I was all in, having filmed about twelve hours of footage for potential use in the sizzle reel. I e-mailed Wendy to tell her what happened. To my surprise, she replied the same day with an alternate plan: "Submit to us through the Discovery Producers Portal. I would like to try and connect you with someone here."

Right away I logged onto the Discovery Producers Portal, and read their submission release. The language wasn't perfect, but I signed the release anyway, and uploaded my one-sheet summary of the Greek show. Discovery was our best shot.

As expected, Callie worked her charm on the normally reticent band of church ladies, convincing the volunteers to let us film their hectic prefestival cooking marathon. Those women were the real miracle workers in my mind, sacrificing long hours to turn out staples of Greek cuisine like stuffed grape leaves and racks of braided sugar cookies known as *koulourakia*.

I filmed the action while Callie interacted with the mostly female cooks. In the tight quarters of the church kitchen, *baklava* came to life: sheets of *phyllo* dough brushed with melted butter, sprinkled with ground nuts, cut in diamonds, and poked with cloves. At a steel table the *dolmathes* were constructed: wet grape leaves splayed, slapped with ground beef, and folded like swaddling babies. My Greek language skills paled in comparison with Callie's, so I was glad to remain behind the camera, and let her banter with the ladies. There was Toula, whose big gold cross dominated the other jewels hanging from her neck; the rascally Ephigenia, who rolled out her *koulourakia* dough with the dexterity and speed of an insect; and snowy-haired Dimitra, who laid down the law on how to prepare a *souvlaki* skewer. "There's a method," she insisted, upbraiding the hapless Callie.

Tucking in and around corners to film all possible angles, I felt alive and in a groove. I was at home among these strong Greek women, who reminded me of the elders I'd grown up with. I knew my father would have been charmed (and shocked) to see me snug behind a camera, roaming the church of my youth. I felt like a part of him was with me.

I WAS SEQUESTERED in the den, in front of my computer, reviewing film footage I'd shot at the Greek festival. My eyes hurt. For the past six hours I had been steeped in images of *souvlaki*, feta cheese, and festivalgoers dancing or throwing back shots of *ouzo*. The abundant film footage had to be time-coded and logged thematically, so as not to waste time in the edit room. All those images of food must have filtered down to my stomach, because now it was growling. I went downstairs to prepare dinner.

"Mom?"

The shadowy foyer was disconcerting. I flipped on a light, and then did the same in the formal sitting room, stopping. My mother had closed all the shutters. But the sun hadn't gone down. Something was wrong. The energy in the house was way off.

Creeping into the darkened family room, I made out the back of my mother's head in front of me. She was watching television in total darkness, with the sound on mute.

"Mom?" I dreaded these encounters, where my mother seemed in a state of hypnosis.

I lowered myself next to her on the couch. "Are you okay?"

"I just feel really sad," said my mother. "I don't know what the future holds for me."

"Well… you could go back to your volunteer work." I paused. "It's been five months, Mom. You can't go on like this. Why don't you go back to the White House?"

"Your dad and I used to drive in together on those days," she said. "He would pick me up after work, and we'd go to Clyde's. We would sit at the bar, eat oysters, and talk about our days."

Steeling my nerves, I wrapped an arm around her, and my mother fell against me.

"He said he would never leave me," she cried.

I turned mechanically in her direction. It was the way my mother said it that threw me off: as if she were registering a complaint. I could imagine my father saying that in a romantic way, but not literally, as if he would never die.

"In what context did Dad say that?" My mother was silent. "Why would he say that?"

"I asked him to," said my mother.

My body went rigid. I tried to imagine my mother saying, "Tell me you'll never leave me, Peter. I want to hear you say the words." But it was against everything I knew about her.

When I was a child my mother used to send me off to school with a theatrical flourish, saying, "Remember who you are!" Years later she explained this was meant to remind me to be proud of who I was because there was no one else like me. It was news to me. I thought every little girl blew off caps in the driveway and devoured *Mad* magazine. What happened to the mother who encouraged that? She would have never asked my father to say *I'll never leave you*. That was the request of an insecure Mom, not someone with the self-confidence of my intrepid mother.

I felt bewildered by the idea that I may have misread her in the past, but I didn't have time to wallow in it, because the Mom of the future was sitting here next to me. Did she have some abandonment issues I didn't know about? And why did my father indulge this fantasy? He was a lawyer who lived and breathed facts. What was his side of the story?

I'll never leave you. It was romantic and sweet.

"But you didn't really believe that, did you, Mom?" I said. "I mean, everyone dies."

"But he said he wouldn't leave me, and he did." My mother began to cry, her body quivering against mine. "He left me."

I realized my mother felt betrayed. My father had broken his promise to *never leave* and left her to fend for herself. But she didn't want to do it—or didn't know how to, because since the day she'd gotten married, her entire life was organized around seeing my father at the end of the day. That was his guarantee, and he delivered on his promise until the day he died.

It all made sense. It explained why my mother didn't want to go back to the White House—Dad wouldn't be there to greet her at the end of the day—and the reason for her excessive sleeping, her zoning out in front of the TV and her distaste for conversation. My mother had no incentive to participate in life if Dad wouldn't be there morning and night.

"Mom," I said, blinking away tears, "you've got to go on living. I know it's hard, but you're alive and healthy, and I need you to stick around. You can't *leave me*."

She narrowed her eyes, as if she hadn't considered this angle.

"I can see why you would feel anxious," I went on. "Your whole life has been structured and directed, and now you're on unfamiliar terrain. But lots of people live with uncertainty every day of their lives." *Including me*, I thought.

My mother took it all in without saying a word. I glanced at the bar, imagining my father standing there making drinks for everyone.

"How about a gin and tonic?" I said, drained.

"That would be good," said my mother.

I dragged myself to the bar. My cabernet took the edge off, and Mom's gin and tonic seemed to brighten her mood, because during dinner that night she spun me in a whole other direction.

"I've decided to stop cooking," my mother said, as if making a grand announcement. "I have cooked literally thousands of meals for our family, and now I'm done."

"Okay…" I said, thinking, *you haven't cooked a meal for anyone since Dad died.*

I set down my knife and fork. "Does that include cooking for me?"

"Yes," said my mother.

Ouch. I knew that if my father were still alive, she would have cooked for him once in a while. I guess in her mind I didn't rate a meal.

"Well, I'm happy to cook for both of us," I said, forging ahead. "As long as I'm not working through dinner or dining out with a friend. Then you'll have to cook for yourself."

My mother silently digested my words, like a chess player contemplating her next move. She looked at me directly. "From now on we should plan on going out for dinner once a week."

"That works for me," I said. But her earlier decree about not cooking was still knocking around in my head. "Would you be willing to at least clean up after dinner?"

"Not really," said my mother, without a trace of irony.

"Wow. Okay, then." I took a sip of a wine.

"I've gotten better at cleaning up in the morning," she said.

I laughed. "So that cancels out the dinner dishes?"

"Well, I'll do them if you don't rush me," said my mother.

"Forget it." They would sit there for hours. "I'll do them."

I sat back, mentally forming an adaptive strategy where preparing dinners was concerned. It involved Costco and take-out food. Then I remembered that I wasn't living in LA, so the take-out would have to be picked up, because no one but Domino's delivered to suburbia. We could increase our trips to the bar and grill at the club. That would lighten my load.

Later that night, I e-mailed my sisters with the latest updates. Unprecedented statements had been made. Dramatic turns taken. My sisters were light years away from these raw emotional experiences, and I had to fill them in. But I was growing weary of my reporting and resentful of my role as cataloguer-in-chief. I realized that while my e-mails had started out as a form of grief therapy, now they felt labored, like cries in the dark for help. Help that would never come.

ONCE IN A WHILE my sister Tasha picked up our mother and took her to the hair salon, or out to get a manicure, or to an evening lecture. It was a welcome break for me, but there was no routine in place that I could count on from week to week. I envied her ability to more or less pick and choose when she would play anything resembling a caregiver role, and her ability to walk away from it when she was done.

I kept telling myself that these were our worst days, and that my mother's dependence on me would eventually end. And then one Saturday she gave me hope. Just before her appointment at the Rich Look hair salon, she came to me with a proposition.

"I'd like to try driving there on my own," said my mother.

"Are you sure?" I was thrilled for both of us. Nervous, too.

"Yes," said my mother. "I appreciate your driving me around, but I don't want to bother you every time I need to run an errand."

By now we had replaced her ancient Mercedes with a newer, used Benz. My mother had driven the black sedan a couple of times, while I rode shotgun. She drove slowly, like most seniors, but well enough. What concerned me was her sense of direction. On one occasion she asked about a turn out of our neighborhood, a route she'd driven for years.

"Do you remember where the salon is?" I said, having dropped her off several times.

"Of course," said my mother.

"I'll give you directions, just in case."

I found a scrap of paper and drew out a simple map. The route was three turns out of our neighborhood, and one turn onto the main road. From there it was a straight line to the hair salon. Less than two miles away, all told. I gave my mother verbal directions as a back up, and sent her on her way. Twenty-minutes later, she called from her cell phone.

"I made a left turn on East Jefferson, like you told me to, but I couldn't find the salon."

"Oh, no," I said. "You weren't supposed to make a left. I said go *through* East Jefferson, and the salon would be ahead, on the left. Where are you now?"

"I'm not sure," said my mother.

"Are you parked, or still driving?" I thought, *please don't let her be driving and talking on the phone.*

"I'm in a parking lot."

"Okay, good. What stores are you near?"

"Um… there's a Trader Joe's behind me. And Ritz Camera on my right."

"I know where you are," I said. "Stay there. I'll drive over, and you can follow me to the salon." It was nearby, but my mother would forget my directions the minute she hung up.

"I hate for you to drive all the way over here," she said.

"It's not a problem. I'll be there in ten minutes."

I hung up, eyes moist. It was such a simple route. How could my mother not get it right? And why did she keep getting lost? First it was in Florida, and now it was here in her own backyard.

I drove up to the Federal Plaza, careening through two yellow lights. Entering through the back of the densely packed minimall, I wound past a Dollar Tree store, through rows of parked cars to the lot near Ritz Camera. I searched for the black Mercedes, spotting my mother at the wheel of her shiny new car. My heart sank. She seemed so small and alone. I got out and fast-walked in her direction, and then crouched next to her door.

"Can you roll down the window?" I said, making a reverse pinwheel motion with one hand. I watched in agony as my mother scoured the dashboard for the electric window button. Finally I tugged at the door handle and it popped open. It was unlocked the whole time.

"I'm sorry," said my mother, upset with herself.

Now I felt worse. Her entire life had been a textbook example of competence. As far as I was concerned she didn't need to apologize for anything.

"It's okay," I said. "I'm going to pull up in front of you, and you can follow me."

I ran back to my car. A few minutes later, I drove out of the plaza with Mom on my tail, checking the rear view mirror every few seconds to make sure I hadn't lost her.

"When do you want me to come back?" I said, tense all over when we arrived at the salon.

"I can manage on my own," said my mother. "I don't want to inconvenience you any further."

I reminded her of the route, and told myself she could always call on her cell phone.

Driving back to the house, I felt more despondent than ever. Five months had passed since my father's death, and my mother was still incapable of remembering the most basic information. I worried about her health. I worried about my own.

I halted at a red light, teary-eyed and called Tasha. I needed to hear the voice of someone I loved who had all the background information. The phone rang and rang. *Where is she?* I thought. I hung up and tried Zoë instead. She answered on the second ring.

"Hey!" said Zoë. "What's going on?"

"It happened again."

"What? What's wrong?"

"Mom got lost going to the hairdresser. I drew her a map, gave her verbal directions—she's been there so many times. I don't understand. Something's wrong with her brain."

"It must be the grief," said Zoë. "Don't you think?"

"I don't know what to think," I said, sniffling. "I feel like I should take her to a neurologist. But I don't have time. And I'm doing so much already."

"I know," said Zoë. "I wish I was there to help you."

"Me too. God, this is so hard. I feel like I'm drowning." My hands were shaking.

"I'm going to book you a massage," said Zoë.

"But I can't—"

"I'll pay for it," Zoë said. She paused. "I hate to say it, because I know you're swamped, but I think you should take Mom to the neurologist. When it's convenient for you."

"There's never a convenient time," I said. "I'm running on fumes here."

"I know… but there's no rush. Nothing's going to change overnight. At least wait until we pass the six-month mark." She meant six months from my father's death.

The traffic light turned green. I made a left into the neighborhood.

"Are you there?" said Zoë.

"Yes. I just—I can't talk anymore. I feel sick."

"I'll call you later to check in," said Zoë. "I love you."

I hung up without a word.

10

Lights, Cameras, Action

Seven months since Dad's death.

I'M BUDGETING FOR speeding tickets now, averaging one ticket per month. There are traffic cameras everywhere in suburbia, quietly passing the day raising funds for the state of Maryland. By the time I see the speed limit signs, I've already gone past them. I sweat out the next two weeks hoping I don't get a notice in the mail. When my ticket inevitably arrives, I feel deflated, and think, *again?* But there is proof of my transgression: a grainy, ghost-like image of the back of my car, with the license plate in full view. Scrutinizing the photograph, I think *what was I doing that day? I wonder where was I going?* Because every day is a blur, and I'm always in a rush.

On a mission to get the Greek show produced, I called the other company Wendy, our ally at Discovery, had mentioned at Starbucks. The head of development couldn't take my call, and I declined to leave a message. *Screw it*, I thought, *I'm just going to go over there.* After the fiasco with Pop Media, all bets were off. I found the address for Reed Street Productions online and showed up unannounced, with a copyrighted one-sheet summary of the Greek show.

"Can I help you?" said the twenty-something working feverishly amid the cubicles of Reed Street Productions.

A few of her colleagues broke stride, eyeing me like a bear on the loose. I gave my name and then dropped Wendy's name, which seemed tacky, but it was a card I had to use.

"Yes," I said. "I'd like to chat for a few minutes with your head of development, Elaine."

"She's in a meeting right now," said the girl.

In the distance I saw a circle of people sitting in a glass-enclosed room. "I can wait."

"We're really busy here," said the girl. "Is there something I can help you with?"

"Sure. I'm developing a new show around Greek food and culture, and—" I handed her my 9 x 12 envelope—"well, it's all in here. If you could just make sure Elaine gets it, I'd appreciate it."

"I will," said the girl, eyeing the exit.

I thanked her and left the office, sapped and chastened. Certain my one-sheet summary would end up in a slush pile, because that was what happened in offices like this.

I don't know why I thought my Reed Street ambush would work. In keeping with the whole topsy-turvy experience, my follow-up messages to the company went unanswered, resulting in a kind of existential defeat. I crossed them off my list. Two of the three big production companies in town were now eliminated as potential partners. I barreled ahead anyway. I just needed one executive to say *yes*. Final editing on the sizzle reel had been completed in late May, and I was proud of what we'd accomplished. The video playfully conveyed the flavor of our show, with vintage, home movie clips and present-day footage of Greek cooking, dancing and dining. The narration explained what viewers would see from one week to the next.

When we scored a pitch meeting at Discovery, I was overjoyed. Then I realized I'd forgotten to address the need for my mother to see a neurologist. The six-month deadline had come and gone, and I hadn't made the appointment. I chalked up the oversight to medical appointment fatigue. At least my mother wasn't having hallucinations or leaving magazines in the refrigerator.

LATE IN THE MORNING on the day of the pitch meeting, I opened my mother's bedroom door. The sight of her lying in bed saddened me. "Mom, I'm going to my meeting at Discovery."

"Good luck," she said, without turning around.

I paused, wistful. "Don't stay in bed too long."

"Mmm-hmm."

I closed the door. I had to psych myself up for this meeting.

Driving my convertible with the top down always brightened my mood. I rolled off the driveway, heading out of the neighborhood with the sun overhead.

Thanks to my newly purchased GPS, I found the way to Discovery Communications without winding up in

Pennsylvania. My writing partner, Callie, was standing in front of the brick office building when I arrived. I parked and cut toward her, squinting at the glass door entrance.

"Here we go," I said, nervous.

"God, I hope this goes well," she said. "How's your mom?"

I threw open the glass door. "Don't ask."

We had arrived early, so after announcing ourselves at the front desk, we waited in the cafeteria. The high-ceiling lunchroom was empty. I felt marooned. To pump myself up, I recited our show's log line and synopsis, repeating them like a mantra. The stakes seemed higher because our insider, Wendy, wouldn't be at the meeting. Booked into another one at the last minute, she had arranged for us to pitch our show to one of her colleagues, an executive producer at Discovery.

Finally, the executive came into the cafeteria and escorted us up a long staircase. He was in his midthirties, tall and curly haired. He shot through the industrial facility like a running back through an open field. I fell into his rhythm, channeling my inner New Yorker.

"Who do you see as the audience for your show?" said the executive as we entered his cramped office filled with scripts and DVDs.

"Anyone interested in ethnic food and culture," I said. "And healthy eating."

"The Mediterranean diet is really popular," said Callie.

"Did you get our one-sheet summary?" I asked.

"Uh… I think so," said the executive, facing his computer. "Let me double-check."

"I'll give you the synopsis," I said. "A Greek-American mom hunts down the secret ingredients in timeless Greek recipes, determined to keep her pride off the kitchen floor and live up to cultural expectations set by her non-Greek friends. Old and new worlds collide as she gets tips from her Greek community, including cagey *Yia Yias*—grandmothers—who take pleasure in her ongoing mishaps while offering unsolicited advice on all aspects of life." I paused, out of breath. "We call it a food and cultural odyssey of epic and comic proportions."

"I can't find the document," said the executive. "But let's take a look at your reel."

He couldn't find the document. Because he was disorganized? Because it hadn't been sent to him? I handed him the sizzle reel DVD. He popped it into a tray on his computer tower.

"Can we watch it on that?" I said, pointing to the television set against a wall. I wanted him to see our video the way a viewer would.

"The DVD player on it is broken," said the executive. "I don't even know why it's in here."

I shifted in my seat, bothered. As the sizzle reel played on his desktop, I tried to gauge the executive's reaction. But he was all poker face. When the piece ended, he swiveled in our direction.

"We might have to shoot some more footage before taking it to Studios," he said.

Before taking it to Studios. Meaning the in-house production unit at Discovery. Future talk—that was promising.

"And we could shoot in different parts of the country," he added, "to open it up."

"Right—and get the local variation on Greek standards," I said.

"You know down in Texas they're going to throw a few jalapenos in that gyro," said Callie.

"Do you have a treatment?" asked the executive.

"We do," I said. "I can e-mail it to you."

"Great." He stood up, all smiles. "I'll get back to you after I've had a chance to review it and talk over the options with Wendy."

I stood on cue. "Thanks for seeing us. I look forward to hearing from you."

Callie echoed my words, and the two of us found our way out of the building.

"I need to revise the treatment," I said, "to include that idea about shooting around the country and getting the local variations on Greek food."

THE NEXT DAY I E-MAILED the executive the revised treatment, alternately excited and on edge as I contemplated what would happen next. And then, when I didn't hear from him after a week, my excitement waned and my stress level shot up. I took to drinking an extra glass of wine at night. Distraction took its toll when I was driving my mother to the dentist.

"Oh!" said my mother, jerking awake as I slammed on the brakes and threw an arm across her chest, the way she did when I was a child. "What happened?"

"Sorry," I said, backing up at the intersection. "I didn't see that red light."

I decided to give the Discovery executive one more week to reply before inquiring about the status of our show. Two weeks was a standard waiting period. I had to gut it out.

To alleviate my stress, I began exploring our options beyond DC—something I'd been putting off, worried about how it would affect my mother if I produced the show out of town. But I owed it to myself (and my bank balance) to knock on every door. I e-mailed the treatment and sizzle reel to a friend who worked at a film editing company in New York. We had known each other since my early days of living there, when I supervised a big editing project for Hearst Entertainment. When she e-mailed a few days later to say she loved the whole concept of the Greek show, I felt vindicated. She planned to discuss our show with a friend who was chummy with one of the producers on *Chopped*, the popular competition show.

TWO WEEKS WENT BY without any word from Discovery. The waiting was torture, reminding me of the agony of decades past, waiting for replies after sending out screenplays. But I was younger then, and able to distract myself with other writing projects or jobs taken to put food on the table. Now I was middle-aged and obsessed with getting just one show produced, and I had the "luxury" of not having to work to put food on the table—though I was (ironically) in charge of buying and serving that food.

I sent the Discovery executive a "checking in" e-mail. To my surprise he replied the same day: "Sorry for the delayed response. I did receive the treatment. Let me review it and get back to you." I was put off by his breezy tone, but forwarded the e-mail to Callie, and prayed that my New York contact came through. I turned to the other big project in my life: caring for my mother.

By now it was not a stretch to say that she had morphed into a Velcro Mom. Thanks to my everyday presence and can-do attitude—which I realized was a duplicate of hers in my childhood—I'd become my mother's companion of choice. I had only myself to blame, but the situation unnerved me. I wasn't used to being joined at the hip with anyone, let alone a grief-stricken, octogenarian mom. It seemed like she was always pushing my limits, in subtle, clever ways.

"Does this appeal to you?" she said one day, sliding a newspaper cutout toward me, about a lecture on Greek antiquities.

"Uh… no."

"Too bad," said my mother, shoving aside the squib.

"Why don't you go with one of your friends?"

"It won't be as much fun," my mother said.

"Mom," I said, "we're not married"—blurting it out unconsciously.

I realized that at times it felt like we *were* married. After months of living together, my mother and I had fallen into a couples-like rhythm, often dining and watching TV together.

"Mom, you need to socialize with someone else besides me," I said, freaked out, pushing her away. Which was ironic, given that I'd spent so much of my life searching for a partner. But I never expected it would be the woman who raised me.

One night, before I went out to meet my high school friend Toni for drinks, my mother preempted my departure with the question, "Are we watching anything special on TV tonight?"

By now we had signed up for Netflix and bought a forty-inch, flat screen TV—all I needed to unleash the movie buff monster in me. I had fun orchestrating our little film festivals, but when my mother began asking every night what was on the bill, I realized I'd made a monster of her, too.

"I'm going out," I said, feeling guilty as usual, leaving her alone. I wondered if my father felt this way when he went out to play a round of golf.

"Why don't you call your friend Maria and have her over for dinner?"

"No," said my mother. "I like talking with her on the phone, but I can't be bothered to cook." She coolly flipped the page of her magazine. "I don't mind being alone."

"What will you eat?"

"I don't know," said my mother. "Maybe I'll just have a cup of soup."

What a dreary image that was. And I knew the whole time I was out, my mother would be watching the clock, waiting for me to come home. Which meant it would be impossible for me to truly relax.

As expected, I glanced at my watch every now and then at Clyde's, wondering how my mother was faring at home. But the evening turned out well. Toni had brought along a pal who used to produce documentary films, and she was captivated by my description of the Greek show.

"You should get in touch with my friend Ken," she said. "He runs an edit facility in DC, and they're looking to change their business model to include coproducing TV shows."

"And we need a coproducer," I said, lighting up.

"I owe him a call. I'll give him a heads-up about your project, then you can call him."

"That would be great."

Things were looking up. I e-mailed Ken the next day.

I DON'T KNOW WHAT I expected to find out at my physical exam that I didn't already know: that every day felt like a race and the finish line was nowhere in sight. I just wanted to get through the exam so I could cross it off my To-Do list. As far as I was concerned, the only remedy for my "sickness" was moving out of the house. I loved my mother dearly, but I now realized that in committing to live with her for a year, I'd had no idea what I was getting myself into. I kept scrambling to advance my career, but it turned out that caring for my mother was a career of its own.

On the day of my physical exam, I scribbled my name on a sign-in sheet, depressed by the familiar, antiseptic waiting room. I could already hear myself telling the doctor that I felt fine, even though most days I was all over the map emotionally. Not to mention that I had definitely gained a few pounds in the last seven months from consuming too much alcohol and eating food I didn't normally eat (like pizza delivered from Domino's) so I didn't have to cook.

I presented my driver's license to the young woman behind the reception desk.

"Do you have your ID?" I asked my mother, there for her check-up with Dr. Post. Our doctors were in the same practice group, so we checked-in at the same place.

"Oh, we don't need hers," said the woman behind the desk.

Taken aback, I realized I had brought my mother in so many times, she was now a VIP.

"Mrs. Panarites?" said the nurse with the tight hairdo, approaching my mother. "Hello, my beautiful."

And she has a fan base, I thought. "I'll meet you back out here," I said to my mother.

"Okay, dear." She gave the nurse a solicitous smile, and latched onto her right arm for balance, as she routinely did with me. It actually made me jealous.

I sat in a coffee-stained, cushioned chair and began scrolling through the e-mails on my BlackBerry. My eyes widened at a message from Ken, the senior editor and part owner of the editing facility in DC. He was able to meet with Callie and me tomorrow. As I was replying to his e-mail, I heard someone calling my name.

"That's me," I said, half looking up as I clicked Send.

Soon after I was shown into an examining room, a freckled-faced woman in her thirties came in and introduced herself as Dr. Brosnan. Her intensity conveyed the impression that while she was in high demand, she was all ears for my allotted time.

"When did you last have a physical?" she said checking my chart, newly established, I assumed.

"I couldn't tell you," I said. "Maybe a year ago?"

"How are you feeling?"

"Okay, all things considered. My sister may have told you our father died."

"Yes, I'm sorry," said the doctor. She put down the chart. "Do you have any concerns about your health?"

"No." I felt distracted. "I'm more concerned about my mother."

"Well, let's see how you're doing, first," said Dr. Brosnan. She began playing hopscotch on my back with her stethoscope. "Deep breaths," she said.

I stared at the floor, inhaling and exhaling like a lung machine.

"All good," said the doctor, throwing off her ear plugs. "Lay on your back for me, please."

I stretched out on the papered table and the doctor began poking around my midsection.

"Why are you worried about your mother?"

"I think something's wrong with her brain," I said, talking to the ceiling.

"How old is she?"

"Eighty-one, now."

"Okay," said the doctor. "You can sit up." She leaned against a white cabinet and made some notations on my chart.

I swung my legs over the table. "Her memory is really bad."

The doctor clicked off her pen, and wrapped her arms around her clipboard. "Can you give me some examples? By the way, your vital signs are normal."

"Great. Well, most of the time she doesn't know what day it is unless she looks at the newspaper."

"That's common for her age," said Dr. Brosnan.

"And she loses her glasses all the time. Last week I looked for them all over the house. Then I realized I'd seen them on the table at the restaurant when we were out for dinner, so I called, and—sure enough they were there."

"So far I haven't heard anything unusual," said the doctor.

"Hmm. I was going to take her to a neurologist."

"That's not a bad idea," said the doctor. "It's possible there is some deterioration in her brain. Cognitive testing would at least establish some parameters."

"If my mother has dementia," I said, panicky, "will I get it, too?"

"Well, remember you have two parents," said Dr. Brosnan. "So you're working with two different sets of genes."

"Which means I could also have a heart attack, like my father," I said.

"Again, two sets of genes."

"Great. So I'll get dementia or I'll have a heart attack."

"Or neither one of those things will happen," she said. "There are many factors to consider."

Of course. Why didn't I think of that?

"Oh—one other thing," I said. "Do you think it's safe for my mother to drive?" Self-consciously, I added, "The last time she went out she got lost, so I started hiding her car keys."

I wasn't used to employing such subterfuge with my mother, but the fact was she had an impulsive side, and some disasters could be avoided.

"At this point she probably shouldn't be driving," said Dr. Brosnan. "And hiding the keys is a good idea. So"—she opened the door—"you're in good health, and I think you're dealing adequately with your father's death. Just keep doing all the things you're doing, and you'll be fine."

Excellent, I thought. *Do you want to buy a TV show?* I followed the doctor out the door. At least my odds for surviving the year, health-wise, looked good.

"I saw in your chart that you don't have medical insurance," said Dr. Brosnan, "so I'll just charge you forty dollars." She handed me a piece of paper. "You can pay at the check-out window."

"Thank you," I said, shocked.

"Take care of yourself," she said, her white coat flying up as she sped away.

ONCE MY MOTHER AND I returned home, I went into action. A while ago her primary care physician had mentioned the name of a neurologist in the building next door, saying that at some point cognitive testing might be useful for my mother. I found the neurologist's phone number on the Internet and prepared myself for a tough conversation with Mom.

It was late enough in the day for me to justify a cocktail, so I went to the bar in the family room and opened the fold-down ledge, flush against the wall. I peered sadly into the kitchen, reminded of my father. He had designed the cut-out bar with flaps on either side of the wall, so you could see into the kitchen if both flaps were down.

I removed the bottle of Johnny Walker Black from the bar ledge and poured myself a scotch on the rocks. Then I made my mother a Tanqueray and tonic.

I sat across from her in front of the fireplace. I didn't want to start in on the topic of brain scans right away, so after we clinked glasses I shared the positive results of my check-up.

"I'm so glad you had a good report," said my mother. "I wish I could say I was in the same shape." She paused, setting down her glass. "I lost my compass."

It was such a poetic way of expressing how she felt. I thought, *dementia patients don't think that way, do they?*

"Maybe that's why you've been having problems with your memory," I said.

"I just... I feel so out of it," said my mother.

"I think you should see a neurologist."

My mother drew back. "Do you think so?"

"You might as well," I said. "We've been to every other doctor on the planet."

She took a drink of her cocktail. "That is so good. Well… if you think I should go, I will."

I went into the kitchen and returned with my monthly planner, gazing at the month of June.

"Huh…. I forgot you have an appointment with Dr. Shanker next week."

"What's that about?" said my mother.

Shanker, I thought. *Which one was that?* "Oh—the dentist," I said. "He has to repair the crown that fell off at the back of your mouth." I scratched my neck, undone by the fact that I was an expert on my mother's inner workings. "I'll make your neurology appointment for the week after that."

"That's fine by me," said my mother.

I KEPT TELLING MYSELF it was only a matter of time before everything fell into place. All I needed was one executive to commit to the Greek show, and I had yet to hear a *No*, so the possibility of a *Yes* still existed. But as the month of July crept in, it seemed our show was slipping away. Though our meeting with Ken—the bigwig at the DC editing facility—had gone well, the reception was different when we met with Ken's business partner.

"We have to be selective in the kinds of shows we develop," said the balding businessman, in between condescending remarks about how the entertainment business worked.

"Did you have a chance to look at the sizzle reel?" I said.

"No."

Things went downhill from there. I realized the guy had already decided our show was a bad bet, and this meeting was just a formality.

Sandwiched in between those ultimately fruitless meetings was fifteen days' worth of e-mail exchanges with my contact in New York. Calls with the *Chopped* executive were set up, postponed, and attempts were made to reschedule. I felt like I was chasing a tornado. Finally I just e-mailed the sizzle reel and one-sheet summary to her assistant, who put it in front of her boss. Eight days later I read the verdict: she loved the idea of *Ouzo, Olives, Opa!* but couldn't grasp the format of the show, based on our reel. That was our only shot and apparently we blew it.

When I finally heard from the executive at Discovery—a month after our pitch meeting—he explained that he'd asked around at the various networks and couldn't get anyone to bite on our program. "Please feel free to get in touch with me about this or other ideas," he wrote.

His laid-back tone made me nauseous.

I wasn't sure what to do next. I didn't want to abandon the work I'd undertaken so enthusiastically because it was exhilarating even when it was crazy-making. But my hourglass was draining fast. Six months had gone by since I'd moved in with my mother, and I still wasn't producing an income. Still, I knew that could change in an instant. The way the entertainment business worked, I could get a call out of the blue from some executive, saying, "Hey—you remember that Greek show you pitched us? We'd like to shoot a pilot."

And I wasn't a quitter. I decided the best thing to do was to put the Greek show on hold and jump into developing our next project. My writing partner and I had already started mapping out the elements of a food-based competition show involving college-age students. The show was straightforward and accessible. A sure thing if there ever was one.

11

The Unbearable Lightness of Tuscany

Eight months since Dad's death.

IT WASN'T UNTIL I WAS IN the van and on the way to Dulles airport that I realized how badly I needed a vacation. And yet, when the idea of flying to Italy for my cousin's wedding had surfaced back in January, I told my mother I couldn't go. She wasn't too keen on the trip either; traveling overseas without Dad would be a monumental *first*. But my mother was open to persuasion.

"I would go if you went with me," she said, foreshadowing her attachment to me in a way I completely missed at the time. "And don't worry about the cost. I'll pay for it."

"That's really generous," I said, "but I can't think that far ahead." The wedding was then six months away. "And I have to focus on earning a living."

The subject of the wedding had come up periodically since my father's death, always in terms of a dilemma, because the trip had been planned when Dad was alive. Going to Italy without him was inconceivable. But a wedding in Tuscany *was* a wedding in Tuscany. My sisters were inclined to go, and my cousin Margo, whose sister DeAnna was the one getting married, was making the trip with her family.

In February, after the historic snowfall, I rethought my attitude. Our house was perpetually dreary and I dreaded the afternoons, when the sun fell quickly. I needed something to look forward to. I told myself I could work flat out until July and then take a break. Maybe the trip would restore a sense of normalcy to our lives, reviving my father's spirit of adventure and love of spending time together as a family.

"We should go to the wedding," I said to my mother one wintry day after shoveling snow for the umpteenth time. "But I'm paying my own way."

"You'll do no such thing," she said. "I have the money and I want to see you enjoy it while I'm alive."

"Mom, you're not going to die any time soon."

"Well, most of my life is behind me," she said.

I was alarmed by her blunt assessment. I realized my mother was more prepared for her death than I was. That was the worst part.

The weeks leading up to our departure had been a whirlwind of nonstop activity. Besides working up a summary of the new TV show I was developing with Callie, I had packed in several extra physical therapy sessions for my mother to prepare her for the cobblestone streets of Italy. And then I accidentally created another time-consuming project for myself.

"How did you sleep last night?" I said, driving her to a physical therapy session.

"Not well," said my mother. "The bed feels so big."

"Why don't we buy you a smaller one?"

"I would like that," said my mother.

"Do you want something traditional, like you have now, or more modern?"

"I don't care," said my mother. "You decide."

"Mom, you have to participate," I said, tired of making all the decisions. "I'll show you some pictures and you can make a choice."

I was determined to improve my mother's quality of life, in any way possible. I went to the website for Crate & Barrel, zeroed in on a sleek, mahogany platform bed, and showed the photograph to my mother. Sold. I scheduled the delivery for after we came back from Italy, and arranged for a new mattress to be delivered the same day.

Before we left for Italy, I managed to get an appointment with the neurologist for an initial consultation. A slim man with a walnut-shaped face and oval eyeglasses, the neurologist appeared to be in his midseventies, although his demeanor was spry almost to the point of being cavalier. I wasn't quite sure what to make of him, but I was pleased that my mother was getting some professional attention where her brain was concerned. For her part, Mom was ready and willing to proceed with the game plan. The neurologist put her through a "minimental" exam—a pop quiz involving such tasks as counting backward and naming the current president—and then (presumably based on my mother's spotty responses) he suggested it would be a good idea for her to get an electroencephalogram (EEG) and a magnetic resonance imagining (MRI). The neurologist also recommended that my mother be given a neuropsychological exam, where she would undergo a rigorous set of written and verbal exercises.

"We might as well cover all the bases," he said.

I didn't see any reason to disagree with him.

Soon after this I took my mother to get two separate brain scans, steering us in and out of waiting rooms, presenting ID cards, filling in forms for her to sign at the bottom. I helped her change into a gown, and then watched with apprehension as my mother was sucked into an MRI tube and bombarded with loud, shrill sounds. I couldn't stay for the hour-long EEG exam; I had to do our grocery shopping. I picked up my mother afterward.

"Did they give you a sedative?" I said, jarred. She looked semiconscious.

"No," said my mother, "but it took forever. I want a reward."

"I'll make you an ice cream cone when we get home."

"That sounds delightful," my mother said.

I glanced at her disheveled hair. "What did they do to you in there?"

"Measured my head, put cream on it, attached all these little plugs with wires."

The image was disturbing, like my mother was part of some mad science experiment.

Days later, when the neurologist called to tell me there was no evidence of Alzheimer's or any other form of dementia in the brain scans, my eyes welled up with joy. But there was one more hurdle: the neuropsychological exam that my mother had undergone. When I dropped her off for that three-hour ordeal, she looked at me with puppy dog eyes and said, "Don't forget me." The guilt I felt for putting her through all those tests escalated my stress. But I wanted to understand what was going on with her brain. Unfortunately the results of her cognitive test wouldn't be available until we got back from overseas, so I had to wait until then for the final piece of the puzzle.

I was anxious to board the plane and be transported to another world, where I could forget about appointments and indulge myself in ten days worth of Mediterranean bliss.

My mother and I left for the airport on a blistering day in mid-July. Inside the air-conditioned taxi, I rechecked the contents of my carry-on luggage to make sure I'd packed our passports, the Euro notes, global phone, and folder I'd assembled with maps, hotel and rental car confirmation e-mails all printed out. As we hit the Dulles toll road, I turned to my mother staring out the window.

"Did you call Awa?" I said. I had suggested she call the bereavement counselor before we left because I knew the trip would be emotional, given all her trips to Italy with my father.

"No." My mother took a tissue out of her sleeve and dabbed at her eyes.

"Why? You told me it was comforting to talk with her."

"I know," said my mother. "I just never got around to it."

I shook my head, frustrated. But I couldn't force my mother to get help.

"We're going to have a good time," I said, convincing myself as much as her. "It will be different, but it will still be fun."

"I hope so," said my mother.

Our overnight flight to Rome touched down at 8:30 a.m. on a Friday. I never slept well on planes, and logged no more than two patchy hours of shuteye on our trans-Atlantic journey. When the jet doors opened, I deplaned in a sleep-deprived haze.

"This way," I said, leading my mother through the soft morning light inside Rome-Fiumicino airport.

My sister Zoë had coordinated her flight from Florida to arrive in Rome at roughly the same time as ours, and we had planned to meet up at the Hertz Rental Car counter. I was getting the keys to a hatchback when I saw her enter the room, with a U-shaped pillow around her neck.

"You're here!" I sped to my sister, relieved to be getting help with our mother.

"Here I am...! And who's this beautiful lady?"

"Zoë!" my mother cried out with a smile.

I led the way to the Hertz parking garage. The low ceiling and balmy air made me claustrophobic. I wanted to get out of there quickly. Zoë and I loaded the luggage into our rented Volkswagen, while Mom climbed into the back seat and conked out.

I fled the garage, searching for the A1 roadway to Cortona, the location of the wedding. The sign for the A1 was ahead. I followed it to the roadway.

All around me aggressive Italian drivers weaved across the asphalt. I tightened my fingers on the steering wheel, afraid I'd be knocked off the road.

"You need to stay awake," I said to Zoë.

"I'll try," she yawned, glancing at the MapQuest directions I had thrust upon her.

I pitched the car forward for the hundred-mile drive north.

The view of the countryside was the only thing that kept me awake, sky everywhere above a vast uneven landscape dotted with cypress trees and stone farmhouses in yellow fields. Mesmerized, I thought, *I wonder if I could live here?* The country was tranquil in a way I longed for, and it felt like home—more so than the place I called home in Maryland, or anywhere else I'd lived. But I wasn't sure where home was anymore. Was it the place where I was born? Or the cities where I'd lived my adult life? I *had* entertained the idea of living in Italy, on my drive from California to Maryland. But that was when I was unattached. Now I was weighed down, managing the house and my mother. I glanced at her in the mirror, thinking *what about Mom?* I told myself I was too tired to think clearly. I should enjoy where I was now. Stay in the moment. *Stay awake.*

Two groggy hours later, I turned off the road at the sight of a rusty sign for the Relais Borgo San Pietro, the villa where I had booked two rooms: one for Zoë and I to share, and an adjacent room for my mother. We were the only family members staying here, which I was glad for. Given the strong personalities in my family, and everyone's different needs, it was better to fan out.

The steering wheel rocked in my hands as we wobbled over a dirt road to a gravel pathway, flanked by low, stone walls. I gaped at our lodgings ahead: a restored, seventeenth-century farmhouse, hidden in the fields.

"Oh. My. God," said Zoë. She turned to me. "Dude."

"Mom, we're here," I said gleefully, watching her eyes widen at her surroundings.

"Oh, gosh," she said. "Isn't this lovely."

I parked and stepped out onto the gravel, overcome by the fresh scent of lavender bushes planted all around the circular driveway. I had read that, at its founding, the villa was a resting place for travelers from all over Europe on the pilgrimage to Rome. I was happy to end my journey here.

Inside the lobby, a radiant concierge greeted us with *buongiornos* and introduced herself as Silvia. She requested our passports, and efficiently checked us in as I took in the décor. Red ceramic tiling filled the floor under an enormous Persian rug. Overhead was a wood-beamed, alabaster ceiling. To the right of the reception desk, a stone portal led to an outdoor patio where we were told breakfast could be taken. Silvia assured us the staff was there to assist us, whatever our needs. I needed sleep. The luggage was brought up to our room, and I flopped into bed.

LATE IN THE AFTERNOON I drove us all into the village of Cortona, jet-lagged but energized by the excitement of our arrival. Cars weren't allowed in the hilltop village, so I parked below it in an area paved with slabs of ancient stone. I knew it would take a while for my mother to negotiate the steep climb into town, but I didn't mind. For once I wasn't in a rush.

We began our ascent. At the top of the hill, the medieval town unfolded in front of me like a secret world. Sunlight flooded the square. Wrought-iron lanterns poked out of stone-encrusted walls, and flower boxes accented windows. The setting didn't seem real. For a moment I just stood there, rapt, by the wide stone steps of the town hall and the watchtower overhead.

I looked back to make sure my mother was okay and saw her behind me, walking on her own. It was strange to see her without my father, but she cut a fashionable figure in her white Lycra top and black jeans, with a kerchief as a belt. And she seemed in good spirits. Seeing her this way eased my lingering tension. I moved into the square, taking in the arched stone walls and arterial passageways. The *siesta* had just ended, and people were milling around but the town wasn't overcrowded.

A familiar figure came toward me. It was my cousin Margo, greeting me with a big wave, as if our meeting in the foreign locale were unplanned. Behind her was my aunt, smiling mischievously at me as she raised a hand above her eyes, shielding them from the sun.

"Where's DeAnna?" I said, hugging Margo and then Thea.

"With the priest," said Margo. "They've been running around all day, finalizing arrangements for the wedding."

"Hey cuz!" Her husband Bill bent to hug me. He was lanky, with a scraggly beard.

We made our way to a café table, round with a glass top and a turquoise tablecloth underneath. Tasha and George were there, as if they had arrived out of nowhere. My mother perked up as more relatives gathered 'round. Family was her comfort zone. Seeing her distracted by them now, I thought, *I might actually get a vacation.*

THE NEXT DAY MY parents' friends Paola and Beppe arrived from Milan. I had never met the middle-aged couple, but had heard about their adventures in Italy with my parents. My mother had met Paola at a cooking class in Cogne, in the Italian Alps. When I wrote to tell her about my father's passing, she called in disbelief. Months later, she booked a room at the same lodge in Italy as ours to offer her condolences in person. I looked forward to adding Paola and Beppe to the social mix; they had memories of my parents that I didn't—memories I knew my mother could take strength from. I was anxious for her to take strength from someone else besides me.

A wave of emotion swept over Paola when she embraced my mother, saying "Helen." Nothing more. Just *Helen.* Her eyes were set close together on a long, symmetrical face, like a Modigliani painting.

My mother held onto Paola with a pained smile. Beppe stepped in and introduced himself to Zoë and me. He was tall and fit, with an impish smile above his close-cropped beard.

The five of us had drinks at a table in front of the villa, interjecting references to my father in between our small talk. I felt an instant kinship with my new friends, but the atmosphere was tinged with sadness. It seemed we were all aware of the one person missing.

LATER THAT NIGHT, Paola and Beppe joined us for dinner at a restaurant in town, hollowed out from a stone wall. Tasha and George met us there, along with his mother Sophia, an aging beauty with a strong inner core, though she was prone to theatrics. Sophia's husband had died at least twenty years ago, but she talked about him so often you would have thought he died yesterday. I guessed it was her way of bonding with my mother, but because I was still torn up about my father, it was hard to endure.

At some point after Paola ordered food for all of us—in Italian, which saved a lot of time—she told me that she was throwing a big party for herself in Milan in November.

"What's the occasion?" I said.

"Ah." She lowered her head a moment, and then turned up, coyly. "My birthday."

"Is it… a special birthday?"

"Fifty," Paola admitted. "You and Helen should come to Milan!"

"We will," said my mother, nodding.

"She'll change her mind," I said to Paola, thinking, *two trips to Italy in one year?* "And I doubt I'll have time. But thank you for the invitation. Maybe Tasha can go with Mom."

I glanced at my sister at the other end of the table, but I didn't think she heard the conversation. She was nodding at something Sophia was saying, as if she was listening, but not really listening. I returned to my *tagliolini*, my mood brightening with each forkful and sip of wine. My mother seemed relaxed, too, nibbling at her bread and cheese as Paola talked about her family.

"My English is not so good," said Paola.

"It's a lot better than my Italian," I said. "So your father must be around the same age as mine. As mine was, I mean."

"Yes, but he is not as nice as yours," said Paola, sounding like a girl with a crush. "*Your* father was warm and kind. And he was very entertaining."

It was funny to hear someone my age talk about my father this way. But I realized Paola saw him as an idealized *father figure*. Dad had his idiosyncrasies, like anyone, but I knew he was an exceptional man.

I was barely into my dessert when George abruptly stood at the far end of the table.

"Right," he said. "Should we go?" He began moving toward the exit.

I drew back, thinking, *why are you telling us when to leave?* I guess he'd had enough of sitting around, and assumed everyone felt the same way. But Zoë didn't look up, deep in conversation with Beppe, and Paola didn't say anything. Then again, she didn't really have to. Her face said it all, with a serpentine smile. Before long Tasha and Sophia were saying their goodbyes. It was strange, like watching people leave the theater in the middle of a movie.

"Pass the bread, would you dear?" said my mother. Clearly not leaving.

I reached for the basket, waving my goodbye. In no rush to go anywhere.

Later that night, when we got back to our lodgings, I checked my mother's pill rack while she was in the bathroom, to make sure she'd taken today's allotment. This was a habit I couldn't break. I was relieved to see the empty slot.

"Do you have everything you need?" I called out, rubbing my eyes, exhausted all of a sudden.

"Yes, dear," said the voice behind the door.

"What are you doing?" Zoë asked, coming into the room.

"Just checking this," I said, fiddling with the pill rack.

"Can I do anything to help?" she said.

"No," I said, edgy. It must have been the jet lag. "But thanks for asking."

THE AIR WAS CLOSE under the scorching summer sun, but I felt rested, having slept well on my half of the bed the previous night. I crunched over the gravel, with Zoë at my side.

"I can drive if you want a break," said Zoë.

We were making a day trip to Florence while Paola and Beppe entertained our mother.

"That's okay." I unlocked our Volkswagen. "I'll drive."

My sister was a fine driver, but I was reluctant to let her drive during any part of the trip. In my mind I was solely responsible for preventing any further catastrophes after my father's sudden death. Between that, my mother's emotional swings, and the myriad breakdowns in our house, it seemed like disaster was always lurking around the corner. I thought if I clung to the wheel now, it would reduce the odds of an accident.

We arrived safely in Florence and found our way to the Piazza della Signoria. The scale of it was overwhelming. It was like an outdoor museum. Statues of robed philosophers stood next to proud, naked warriors. I turned in all directions, spreading my arms like wings.

"Wow," I said, giddy as a kid skipping school.

"Should we go into the museum?" said Zoë, smiling.

I had purchased our tickets for the Uffizi Gallery in advance, and now plucked them out of my bag as we ambled through a long, rectangular passageway. The museum rose up around me in high walls, stone everywhere—rough hewn on the ground, ornamental in the air.

A feeling of reverence came over me. I felt alive in the world, and unencumbered, far from the daily pressure of squeezing thirty-six hours into a twenty-four-hour day. I wanted to stay there all day and night, and never go back to suburbia. It would have been easy to stay, given the staggering collection of art on display inside the famous Renaissance museum. Botticelli, da Vinci, Michelangelo—Italian masters at every turn.

At the end of our tour, I discovered a Caravaggio exhibit in the dungeon-like basement. Standing before the *Medusa*, painted on a curved wooden shield, I was transfixed by the snakes writhing out of her severed head—mouth agape, eyes cast downward in horror. The expression was familiar. Tasha had told me that when she saw our father in the hospital after he died, his mouth was hanging open and his eyes were wide with shock. I realized his expression was the same as that of the *Medusa*: it was the dismay of sudden death.

When I returned with Zoë to Cortona, I felt restored, as if I had regained a sliver of my long-lost independence. In the front of the villa, Beppe and Paola were loading up their SUV. They had checked out and said goodbye to my mother, who was napping in her room. The three of them had spent the entire day in nearby Camucia, strolling into shops and art galleries, having a long lunch.

"Thank you so much for coming," I said. "And for spending time with my mother."

"So, we will see you in November," Paola said. "Helen says you will come."

"Maybe," I replied with a halfhearted smile. It wasn't at the top of my To Do list.

THE NEXT DAY, Margo and her husband Bill had us over for dinner at the flat they were renting in town. Apparently Bill had discovered a cooperative food market in Camucia and returned with fresh ingredients for a pasta dish. I welcomed the invitation. Bill was a talented cook, at home in the kitchen, and their flat had a rooftop view of the medieval town.

"I should wake up Mom," I said, returning from a hike with Zoë.

"I'll do it," she said.

"Oh… okay," I stammered, unused to hands-on assistance. "Make sure she didn't miss any of her pills from breakfast."

"Got it," said Zoë.

"And make sure she wears flats," I added. "It's a steep climb up to that apartment."

I felt anxious, stretched my neck, and let out a deep breath.

Half an hour later, I followed my mother in her heel-less shoes up the twisting, narrow set of stairs to Bill and Margo's flat. I turned into the kitchen, soothed by the citrusy smell of fresh basil.

"Hey, cousin!" said Bill, turning as he lifted a large pot off the stove.

"It smells great in here." I set my bottles of Montepulciano on the counter.

"Thanks. Everyone's outside. DeAnna is with the groom's family tonight, so it's just us. But hey—there's all kinds of food out there. Wine, too."

I stepped out onto the roof, enclosed by leafy cypress trees, beneath an orangey-blue sky. The outdoor dining table was filled with fresh mozzarella, sliced tomatoes, baguettes, fresh salami and olives. Tasha, George and his mother Sophia were sitting at the table, with George on the end. Margo's two teenagers wandered in and out of the flat, passing my aunt, tucked gnome-like into a cushioned bench along the wall. It was odd how we all kept cropping up in the same places, from one day to the next. But now everyone seemed in their own worlds, eating and drinking, without much talking.

I poured myself a glass of wine, doing my best to ignore the feeling that I was at a staged, pop-up event. Behind me I heard a bit of conversation and swung around to see Margo talking with her husband's college friend, Sam.

"Hi... nice to see you." I gave him a hug and Margo, too.

"You too," said Sam, looking all relaxed and summery in linen shirt and slacks.

I had only hung out with him a few times, but I liked Sam. He was in his early forties, smart and with a dry sense of humor. I seemed to recall he was an immigration attorney.

"Oh gosh," said Margo, dashing off. "I almost forgot—I've got to make the salad."

"Make Bill do it," Sam called out, laughing.

"I haven't seen you in a while," I said. "What have you been up to?"

"I just finished the process of applying to the Foreign Service," said Sam with a loopy gaze, as if he had finished the application ten minutes ago.

"Oh." I paused. "Well—congratulations."

I had nearly forgotten this was once my field of study. Only a year had passed since I'd earned my master's degree in public diplomacy, but it felt like a lifetime ago. *My last significant accomplishment*, I thought, shifting uncomfortably.

"I can't believe it's finally over," said Sam. "It took like, a year."

"So… what's next?"

"Orientation in the fall. And then I'll probably get posted to Korea."

"Hmm."

"And you?" said Sam.

"Uh… well, I'm trying to get a couple of television shows off the ground."

"That sounds like fun," he said, tilting his head.

"It is. It could be." I paused. "I don't know."

All of a sudden an aching self-doubt took hold of me. My foray into the world of reality TV seemed like a huge gamble compared with Sam's clear path forward. I realized that since moving in with my mother, the only thing I could honestly say I'd been successful at was taking care of her. I knew I'd been instrumental in keeping my mother alive after my father's death, and this was deeply gratifying. But it wasn't the same as earning a living in a field of my choosing. And I couldn't play the role of caregiver forever. Not if I wanted to do well in another profession.

I felt jittery. The conversation with Sam was playing tricks with my head.

"I had a friend in LA who went into the Foreign Service at your age," I said, unable to let go of the topic, like picking away at a scab. "He was also an attorney."

"Yeah, you know I think the cut-off for applying is pretty late," said Sam. "I think you can apply up to age fifty-nine."

Fifty-nine seemed like a lifetime away. Okay, I was fifty years old, but I had more energy than most people half my age. And I was running out of time, halfway through my year-long commitment to living with my mother. Maybe the Foreign Service could be my way out, a way to ensure my financial future *and* make a clean break from my role as a primary caregiver. The catch was, if I applied to the Foreign Service, I would have to live with my mother longer than I'd intended because of the long application process. But that would give us time to plan the next stage of *both* our lives. And if the results of my mother's cognitive exam were troubling... well, I would adjust accordingly. *We* would adjust—as a family. I had always regretted not finding a way to use my master's degree. But I could still put it to use. *Maybe I should apply*, I thought, agitated and excited at the time.

If only the evening had ended there. An hour or so later, the discussion turned to the next day's activities. Seizing the floor, George's mother, Sophia, announced her intention to spend the day shopping with my mother and my aunt. *Oh God*, I thought. *Here we go*. When Sophia set her mind to something, it was already done. But what about the logistics? Sophia woke up every morning at four or five, and had boundless energy. My mother often slept until 11 a.m. or noon, and became easily overexerted. My aunt woke up anywhere from eleven to one, and moved at the speed of a tortoise. How would all those different paces be lassoed into one?

As I was thinking this through I heard Sophia say, "Jana will drive Helen."

"Wait—what?" I said, snapping to attention.

It was one thing for *me* to decide to drive my mother somewhere, but no one had the right to volunteer my services. Not on my vacation. But now Sophia was on a tear, explaining to everyone that I would drive my mother into town in the morning and escort her to my aunt's lodgings, where the ladies would all meet up.

"What about what I want?" I fumed.

I looked right and left as I waited for my mother or my aunt—anyone—to ask what I thought of this plan. But no one said a word. I felt my face getting hot.

At the far end of the table, George threw up a hand as if calming an angry mob. "Look," he said, "here's how it's going to work. Jana, you'll pick up Helen—"

"Stay out of this, George"—I cut him off, seething—"it has nothing to do with you." Why was he repeating his mother's plan? She didn't say it in Italian.

"That's it," he said. "I'm out of here." He shot out of his chair and into the flat.

I stopped. What was going on?

Sophia stood and gathered her purse. "Well, I knew this would happen," she said. "It always does."

"What do you mean?" I said.

"Never mind," said Sophia, moving off the patio, on the heels of her son.

It all had happened so quickly. I felt alone and ambushed, desperate for someone to come to my defense. But no one did. Zoë was in the kitchen, oblivious to the drama, and my sister Tasha witnessed the scene in silence. Then she got up and scurried away, to catch her ride home.

I found my way downstairs, and stood outside with Margo, Bill, and Sam. They were speed-smoking cigarettes. I summoned every ounce of strength to keep myself from bursting into tears.

"That was weird," said Bill.

"Seems like George has a really short fuse," Sam said.

"He and his mother are very close," said Margo. "If you go against them, they'll hurt you."

I craned my neck up the long stairway to the flat. Why was it taking so long for Zoë and my mother to come outside? Finally they appeared.

"What happened?" said Zoë, confused.

"It's not even worth getting into," Margo said.

We hugged goodbye and trickled down the wide alleyway to the cobblestone parking area. I don't know how I managed to avoid plunging off the road, twisting through the night as I drove out of town, pushing back my tears. Luckily, it was a short distance back to the villa.

When we arrived there, I kissed my mother goodnight, in a fog.

"I don't care what happens tomorrow," she said. "I don't need to go shopping."

I loved her more than ever.

I closed her door, went into the adjacent room, and sat on one side of the bed. I covered my face with my hands and began sobbing.

"I'm so tired."

"Jana, you're doing a great job," Zoë said in a somber tone.

I realized no one in my family had ever openly acknowledged that taking care of my mother *was* a job. And it was much more demanding than any job I'd ever had. Zoë seemed to grasp this. I thought maybe I should talk about what happened. But I was too wrung out.

I knew my tears were disproportionate to the events of the evening, and that at another time in my life I would have made my own decision about what to do the next day.

I hadn't cried so violently since being told of my father's death. I realized that eight months had passed since then, and that grief travels with you, no matter how far you go.

The next morning, I drove my mother a mile up the road. As I pulled into a pebbled parking area, I saw George sitting at the wheel of his rental car, with his mother in the passenger seat. The car was facing out, ready for take off, with the engine running. George had a scowl on his face, as if he had been brooding for hours. I kissed my mother and she transferred herself into his car. George drove the two mothers into town for their day of shopping. I have no memory of how this arrangement came about.

IN THE DAYS THAT followed the rooftop dinner, I mostly kept to myself. Avoidance as a survival tactic worked well for me. I hiked the trails around our lodgings and lounged by the pool. I made a day trip to Sienna with my sisters and mother. And then it was time for the wedding.

Guests from far-off cities assembled in the town of Cortona for the high point of the week. I barely registered their presence, entranced as I was by the interior of the San Niccolò church. The small, fifteenth-century Baroque church had a terracotta floor and rows of timeworn wooden pews, four at the back of the church, and a single row on the left wall near the altar.

All around me were Italian Renaissance paintings. Overhead was a coffered, wood ceiling that seemed suspended in the air.

It was hard not to feel happy in the presence of so much beauty. Standing along the wall, I faced the altar and waited for the service to begin, using my program as a fan in the baking heat.

The sound of wedding music filled the church, light bulbs flashing as DeAnna entered on her father's arm. She was slight but sturdy, with blazing brown eyes. I glanced at my mother, standing at a wood railing facing the altar. She appeared relaxed, but I knew her mind was churning. I imagined her thinking back to the day of her own wedding and the start of her life with my father.

From the brief program it appeared that the ceremony would take no more than an hour. I glanced at the priest, a homely looking man with thick glasses, unkempt hair and sagging jowls. The music faded out, and all eyes set upon DeAnna and Francesco. They knelt before the priest on an upholstered bench, recited their vows and exchanged their wedding rings with covert smiles. When the ceremony ended, the priest encouraged everyone to share in the union by embracing one another. The guests all obliged as if it was a sixties-era love fest. Moments later, order was restored, and the bride and groom faced the altar for a final blessing.

At 6:45 p.m. the ceremony ended, and champagne was served in the gravel courtyard in front of the church. Sunlight pierced the cypress trees, casting a romantic glow over the intimate setting. Speeches were made, and then the wedding party began trickling out of the courtyard. The dinner reception would be held at Osteria del Teatro, a restaurant located on one of the spidery side streets in the center of the town. It was within walking distance from the church, but I didn't know how to get there. We were at the highest point in town, so descent was the only option.

I broke away to move our rental car to a lower level, safe in the knowledge that my mother was surrounded by a bevy of escorts. Afterward, I found my way to the base of a narrow road near the restaurant, and noticed Sam assisting my mother down the hill. Their arms were both raised, as if dancing a minuet. This was something my father would have done.

SCATTERED CONVERSATION filled the air as the wedding party trickled into Osteria del Teatro. Moving inside the arched walls of the restaurant, I watched DeAnna gently steer my mother toward a private room to the right of the entrance, where parents and grandparents would sit with the bride and groom, along with siblings and a few close friends. My mother gave me a little wave. It was wonderful to see her enjoying herself; she had always been a social butterfly, but I hadn't seen that side of her since my father's death.

"You're in there," DeAnna said to me, pointing to the left of the entrance. In a low voice she added, "That's my dream table."

"I can see why."

DeAnna was a sculptor, with an eclectic group of friends, and they all seemed to be in that room: painters, sculptors, academics. I moved inside, found my name card, and wedged into a chair.

"I'm Peter," said the Greek on my right, dressed in a smart-looking, navy blue jacket and yellow print tie.

"Jana," I said. "Nice to meet you." *This is going to be fun*, I thought, champagne tipsy.

"And I'm Mark," said the guy on my left, in the light blue suit and straw pork pie hat. "His partner. For tonight, anyway."

From the sound of his slurred speech I could tell Mark was already plastered. I wasn't sure if I would ever catch up with him, but I was certainly willing to try.

After a raucous dinner, we all moved into the bride and groom's dining room, and a large wedding cake was presented on a platter wreathed in leaves. A single piece of cake was cut for Francesco and DeAnna before the platter was whisked away for cutting into individual pieces. The waiter draped a linen napkin over the top of a champagne magnum, and then leveled the backside of a saber at the neck of the bottle. Gasps and applause filled the room as he sliced off the neck of the bottle without spilling a drop. More champagne was poured. I couldn't remember the last time I felt so happy to be alive. I was achingly aware of how quickly it could end.

12
State of Mind

Nine months since Dad's death.

AFTER WE RETURNED from Italy, I felt more disconnected than ever from my surroundings. The sprinkler-infused lawns of suburbia were no match for the golden fields of Tuscany in my mind. Something inside me had changed. I had a sense of foreboding about my future.

And then one day, during a walk, I realized the future was already here. I stopped in my tracks: my old elementary school had been fully renovated. Nearly a year had passed since I first saw the sign reading "Closed for Renovations." Now there was a new sign on the lawn heralding the arrival of students for the start of the school year. Classrooms were reopening, lives resuming, in a deliberate direction. I realized I was still stuck in first gear—unsure of *my* direction, and where I was heading with my career. I needed to make some changes—now. But where should I begin? My stomach churned with uncertainty. I decided to start small.

Back at the house, I went into my father's workbench area in the basement, and located a pair of pliers. I went into the garage and unscrewed the California license plates from my car, studying the cold metal symbols of my life on the West Coast. I set the plates on the concrete, feeling blue. I told myself to let it go; wherever I called home, it wasn't defined by a license plate. Home was a state of mind. I took the Maryland plates out of my trunk, which had been flopping around in there for four months, and attached them to both bumpers.

Well, that's done, I thought, sobering up and heading briskly into the house. I returned the pliers to the workbench area, gazing at all the tools my father had amassed over the years: screwdrivers, extension cords, drills, little plastic drawers filled with nails in all sizes—it was like a mini-Home Depot in there. The scene pulled me back to my father's past and got me to thinking about my own. I remembered that many years ago I had quit working in television production for a reason: because it was a strenuous, fickle business. So why was I now developing another reality TV show, after failing to get the Greek show produced?

I stared at the linoleum floor, searching for clues in the worn tiles. I had thrown myself into the Greek show to celebrate a world dear to my heart and to share that world with a television audience. But if no executives were interested, it had to end there. Grinding out another reality TV project without getting paid would be a colossal waste of time. If I was going to have any chance of moving out of the house, I had to find a more reliable line of work.

My mind jumped back to the conversation with Sam, in Italy, and the thought of joining the Foreign Service. A picture formed in my head, of wearing pant suits every day. Was that me? A member of the buttoned-down culture of the State Department? *At least do the research*, I thought.

I went upstairs and logged onto the Internet, knee bouncing. I remembered my friend Amy from grad school had done a summer internship at the State Department, and had gone through the process of applying to the Foreign Service. In the end she had decided to move to Arizona instead, but I could learn from her experience. Fingers racing, I clicked into my Gmail account and typed Amy a message: "Let me know when you have time for a quick chat."

"When are we leaving for that appointment?" my mother called out from downstairs.

I looked at my watch. "Now!" I said. "I'll be right down!"

I had forgotten about my mother's neurology appointment. The results of her cognitive exam were back. Now we would get the verdict. I hit *Send*, and sprang out of my chair.

DRIVING TO THE neurology appointment, I thought more about the Foreign Service, doubt creeping in. What if my application was rejected? I *was* fifty years old. I could be dinged for that reason alone. I told myself that was ridiculous; if anything, my age should be an advantage. Age equaled wisdom. And, I had a master's degree in this field. Plus, I had spent most of my life telling stories, which was the heart of public diplomacy: telling America's story to the world.

"I'm thinking about applying to the Foreign Service," I said to my mother, desperate to unclutter my brain.

"That sounds like a good idea," she said. "I'll go with you."

Whoa. "Mom," I said, "we're talking about a job overseas, not a vacation."

"Oh, well," she said. "I guess I'll just stay in the house."

"Uh… that's not going to work."

"Why not?" said my mother.

"Because you can't live alone. The house is enormous. Come on, Mom. Be realistic."

"I am being realistic. Mary Matrakas lives alone in her house." This was a widowed contemporary of my mother's.

"Her house is much smaller than yours," I said. "And she's not there all the time. She's off visiting those grandchildren of hers in Wisconsin."

I turned into the medical building complex, wrenched inside, reminded that my mother didn't have the distraction of grandchildren. None of us had kids. I had long since made my peace with being childless, accepting in my late thirties that the window for getting pregnant was closing and my career was a high priority. I would have had a child with a partner, had I met the right one, but I hadn't, so that was that. My only real regret was that I didn't give my mother a grandchild.

"I visit with people," said my mother, lowering her head.

"I know," I said. But her varied group of friends rarely came around anymore. It was as if my mother's grief had lost its luster.

"We'll figure something out." I pulled into a parking spot, feeling my stress level rising. I wished I had never raised the subject.

Inside The Neurology Center, my mother and I sat across from the doctor with the walnut-shaped face. In his hands were the results of my mother's three-hour cognitive exam performed by a clinical psychologist. I was glad for the in-depth testing; I thought a flesh-and-blood human would be better than any machine at solving the enigma of my mother's brain. I thought, *now we'll get some answers.* To my dismay, we didn't. Not in terms of an actual diagnosis.

"So everything looks pretty good," the neurologist said. "The clinician found that you had no problem with spatial configurations, and that your emotional state was favorable."

"That's strange," I said, "considering how much time Mom spends in bed."

"Well," said the neurologist, "one thing in the report that I did find interesting was that you had difficulty naming things." He studied my mother at length, as if expecting her to try and name her impairment.

"And...?" I said, growing impatient, because it seemed he had made my mother uncomfortable. She turned to me, confused, and then looked at him.

"It's a memory problem of some kind," he said. "But I can't put my finger on it."

"Okay..." I said, thinking, *but aren't you the expert? What was the point of all those tests?*

Frustrated, I listened as the neurologist outlined the options for treatment in the form of two new drugs whose names sounded like newly discovered planets.

"Namenda and Axona have been given to patients in the early stages of Alzheimer's disease," he said. Quickly, he added, "But I'm not diagnosing Alzheimer's."

"Then—I don't understand," I said. "Why are you prescribing these drugs?"

"Because they've been effective in some patients in slowing the progression of memory-related diseases. I'd like to see if they help your mother." He paused. "But there's no guarantee either drug will work."

It took a few moments to get my head around his Orwellian pronouncement: the neurologist was recommending Alzheimer's-related drugs for a patient who hadn't been diagnosed with Alzheimer's, in the hope that one of the drugs may or may not work to correct *a memory problem of some kind.*

"Why don't we do a PET scan?" I said, my mind reeling.

Through research, I had learned that Positron Emission Tomography scans were used to diagnose certain types of dementia. Unlike an MRI, PET imaging revealed how the brain was actually working, not just what it looked like.

"That's an option," said the neurologist. "But it's expensive."

My mother was shaking her head.

"Why do you want her to have it?" he asked me.

"Because I want to know what's happening to my mother's brain," I said. What was wrong with this guy? Wouldn't anyone want to know her parent's state of mind?

"Do you understand your daughter's concern?" said the neurologist.

"Yes," my mother said. "But I don't want any more tests."

I understood her point of view, given all the testing she'd undergone. But I couldn't accept *a memory problem of some kind.* It was much too vague. I slumped in my chair, telling myself that knowing *why* something happens doesn't change *what* is happening.

"In a situation like this," said the doctor, "I usually defer to the patient's wishes. So. Let's start with the Namenda."

He reached into a cabinet and produced a four-week starter kit. As he handed it to me, I imagined a pharmaceutical representative stocking his cabinet weekly with samples of the latest overpriced elixirs. For a moment I felt angry. Then I just went numb.

I split open the kit and examined the weekly timetable set forth via color-coded strips, yellow for the initial 5mg dosage, and green for the increase to 10mg. As I did this the neurologist zipped through his instructions for upping my mother's dosage over time.

"I'd like you to come back in seven weeks," the neurologist said to my mother. He wrote out a prescription, which he handed to me. "This will cover the remaining three weeks of our experiment."

He gave me a concerned look. "How long will you be living with your mother?"

"I'm not sure," I said, flustered. Was there something he wasn't telling me? "I may be applying to the Foreign Service. But I wouldn't be posted for several months."

"That's good," said the neurologist.

"Why? Should I be worried about my mother? Or—should *we* be worried?"

"No, no." The neurologist waved a hand, short back-and-forth movements, like a metronome. "It's just—it's good that you're there."

He turned to my mother. "Are you driving now?"

"No," she said, sitting up. "But I expect to be soon."

"I would prefer that you hold off for a while," said the neurologist. "Some of my patients get behind the wheel thinking they know where they're going, only to find themselves driving around lost for hours. Your reflexes are in a compromised state, which presents an additional safety issue."

I had to admit, I was glad for his words, even if my mother was disheartened by them—which I could tell she was—because I knew she would heed the doctor's advice. She was from the generation that believed doctors were infallible. And I didn't want her to risk getting lost again, like she did going to the hair salon.

"Is it normal to want to block out depressive thoughts?" said my mother.

"It's a common grief response," said the neurologist. "But it's important to remember that in the process of blocking out depressive thoughts, you're not *letting in* positive thoughts and experiences."

A flash of recognition crossed my mother's eyes as she digested this information.

Exactly, I thought, although his words drove home the point that this was one thing I couldn't fix. My mother was the only person capable of reconfiguring her mind.

She seemed imprisoned by it now, but I was sure she could claw her way out. Didn't everyone have the ability to reach for some degree of contentment?

When we returned to the house, I saw that my mother wouldn't be reaching for anything any time soon. She took her first dose of Namenda and climbed into bed. I wondered if the memory pill would cause her to remember things she would rather forget.

I KEPT GOING BACK AND FORTH on whether to apply to the Foreign Service. Half of me knew I should get on with it and apply, while the other half—unsettled by our visit to the neurologist—broke out in a cold sweat at the thought of leaving my mother to live halfway around the world.

"You can always turn down a post," said Amy, my friend from grad school. We were on the phone at around eight in the evening East Coast time.

"That would look bad, wouldn't it?" I said, knotted up inside.

"People do it. I would, if I didn't like where they were sending me. There's really no downside to applying. Except that the process takes, like—forever." Amy laughed.

"That would actually work in my favor," I said. "I'd need time to figure out the best place for my mother to live and convince her it's time to sell the house. Not to mention convincing my sisters and preparing the house for sale."

My spirits sagged, realizing this would all fall on my shoulders. I was the only daughter directly affected by my mother's health and the enormity of the house, which meant I was the only one thinking seriously about making changes in our lives.

"How *is* your mom?" Amy said. "I love her. She's so sweet."

"She's still struggling. But she has her moments. What's hard on me is seeing her sleep all the time. She's on her third antidepressant, but it doesn't seem to be helping."

"I'm sorry," said Amy. "Well, I think you should apply to the Foreign Service. Like I said, you can always turn down a post. The point is, you want to have the option of saying no."

"Right. Thanks." I got off the phone, went downstairs and poured myself a glass of wine, thinking, *one day at a time*. It really did help. The wine, and the cliché.

THE DISPATCHER FROM Crate & Barrel had called about the Asher Queen bed frame I'd ordered for my mother. Apparently the frame was to be delivered today, between noon and 2:00 p.m. A new mattress from the Healthy Back Store was also scheduled to be delivered today. The saleswoman had told me a dispatcher would call by 9 p.m. last night with the estimated time of delivery. But the call never came, so now my mother's bedroom makeover was in jeopardy.

I rushed to her bedroom. It was 9:30 a.m., the crack of dawn for Mom. I knocked on the door, opened it, and leaned halfway into her lair.

"Sorry, but I need to break everything down in here," I said. "The delivery guys from Crate & Barrel are coming at noon, and they won't set up the bed unless this is all cleared out."

"I'll get up right now," said my mother, apparently willing to accommodate any plan that would enhance her sleep experience.

I hurried downstairs and called the 1-800 number for the Healthy Back Store. An unidentified woman connected me to the Rockville location, where I learned the mattress I'd ordered wasn't in the store, but at the warehouse in Beltsville. Transferred there, I was told that I'd been misinformed at the time of my order. The mattress wouldn't be available for another two weeks.

"What?" I said. "Cancel the order. I want a full refund of the eight hundred and seventy-five dollars charged to my credit card."

"Well, are you sure—"

"Look, if there's a prob—put your manager on." I stopped, realizing this was exactly the sort of thing my mother used to say. *Oh my God,* I thought. *I've become my mother.*

"I can do the refund," said the Healthy Back Store lady.

"Thank you. I'll take down the confirmation number for the refund whenever you're ready."

The process finished, I hung up and saw my mother entering the kitchen in her bathrobe.

"Is everything okay?" she asked.

"Remind me again of your must-haves in a mattress."

"It has to be firm," said my mother.

"How firm? Super or medium?"

"I don't care," she said. "You decide."

Of course. Why did I even bother to ask? I rocketed upstairs, stripped the sheets off her king size bed and flopped the mattress and box spring off the frame, leaning them against the plantation shutters. I went down to the basement, found the Black & Decker drill, and went back upstairs. I disassembled my mother's bed frame and lugged the pieces to the basement. Back in the bedroom, I vacuumed the lemon-colored, wall-to-wall carpeting, thinking *Mattress Discounters.* That was my next stop.

I scooped up my car keys in the foyer. "I'm going out!"

"Take it easy, dear," my mother said, from the kitchen.

Two-and-a-half hours later, I was putting fresh sheets on the new bed frame and mattress. I replaced my mother's dated, yellow print quilt with a fluffy, white duvet from California, draping it over the sheets like frosting on a cake.

The finished product was spectacular. I had felt a rush pulling it all together—buying a new mattress under the gun, having it delivered the same day, right after the mahogany bed frame was delivered from Crate & Barrel. I bounced downstairs to find my mother for the unveiling.

"Oh, Jana," she said, as we moved into the bedroom. "It's beautiful!"

"I hope it's not too low to the floor."

"Oh, no." She sat on the duvet. "I love it. Thank you so much."

"You paid for it," I said. "I just made it happen."

"You mean your dad paid for it," said my mother. "Fortunately he left me in good shape, financially."

"Mom," I said, "you built the nest egg together. You were running our lives while Dad was zooming ahead with his career. You *made it possible* for him to leave you in good shape, financially."

My mother smiled. "Maybe."

"You're too modest," I said, shaking my head.

To me one of the reasons their marriage worked so well was because they both had a stake in my father's success. They were equal partners, even though my mother wasn't paid for her labor. That she had also found the time and energy to write, run church committees, and teach Junior Great Books at my elementary school was something that to this day I find astounding. But I realized this was where I got the energy needed to move eleven times, and juggle my own writing with paid work. My mother had passed that gene on to me; it kept me going even now.

THE NEXT MORNING I came downstairs to find a note from my mother written on white legal paper. In the upper right corner of the page she had written: 4:42 a.m.

> *Dear Jana,*
> *Sleepless in Bethesda and my mind racing merrily along. I have decided to hunker down this autumn and write a book "Volunteering at the White House." What say you, my pal, about journeying thru on such a comittment? → sp? xxx → would you be my agent?*

I began crying. That was the spunky Mom I'd been missing, and finally found on the page. I had been begging my mother to write the White House volunteer book for years. But she had always said no, even when I offered to help her with the writing. She saw it as her patriotic duty to keep mum about what she'd seen and heard in the nation's most famous residence. But my mother had told me so many juicy stories and had collected a lot of memorabilia from her White House years, including a seating chart for a birthday lunch for First Lady Nancy Reagan (code name "Rainbow").

I set down the note, my own mind *racing merrily along*. I pictured an activity-filled autumn, starting with taking the Foreign Service Officer (FSO) test on October 6. By now I had signed up to take the exam, and had told my writing partner

Callie about my new course of action. She was gracious and understanding of my need to move away from developing television shows. We continued to remain friends, connected by our Greek heritage and our whirlwind adventure on a labor of love.

Before taking the FSO test, I had to fill out an application at the Department of State website. The online application was an eye-popping twenty-three pages long. And I had taken the unadvisable approach of filling it out in one sitting, which was fine for the multiple choice "About You" questions, but by the end of the "Work Experience" section I was close to passing out. That section required a description of each job I'd had in the past ten years—"paid and unpaid, and volunteer work, internships, or periods of unemployment (of more than one year)." No more than fifteen jobs could be listed. But in the past ten years, I'd had at least twenty paid and unpaid jobs. This got me to worrying about how the review team would interpret my herky-jerky career path. Then I went into a panic over how they would interpret my two-year employment hiatus to attend graduate school full-time. And how I should spin my unpaid work on the Greek food and culture show. And whether I should list my current "job" as caregiver to my mother.

Two hours of handwringing later, I finished the application, and sent it sailing across the Internet. I felt relieved. But I had a nagging concern about my mother's mental state. What if the Namenda didn't work? Or the Axona? Would her health affect my plans?

I researched the State Department policy on bringing family members overseas. The website said that in some cases "a dependent parent may travel with you to your post." What was I thinking? *She can't come*, I thought. *No ifs, ands or buts.*

I told myself the White House volunteer book was the solution. Writing it with my mother would stoke her desire to lead a more productive life. And it would give her confidence to embrace change—defined in my mind as agreeing to sell the house and moving into a smaller set-up. If I could just convince my mother to do this by the time I finished applying to the Foreign Service. That was my goal. And the volunteer book would give me something to do during that drawn-out process. I had never written a book, but it was a lifelong desire. Now I could do it with Mom.

I mapped out a schedule. The results of my Foreign Service exam wouldn't be available until late October. While I awaited the results, I would conduct a series of taped interviews with my mother in the manner of an oral history project. The material would eventually be shaped into a manuscript, interspersed with photos and reprinted memorabilia. *The memorabilia will jog her mind*, I thought, convinced the items would trigger anecdotes that could be shaped into a story. I would just have to be patient with my mother and ask her lots of questions.

Assuming I passed the Foreign Service exam, in early November I would put the White House book on hold and turn to the next stage in the application process: composing my personal narrative essays for the Qualifications Evaluation Panel, a three-person review panel charged with identifying the best matches for each career track—in my case, public diplomacy. After reviewing my essays, online application, and exam results, the panel would invite me in for an interview, also known as the Oral Assessment. I stopped, palms sweaty. What if they didn't invite me to the interview? But that wouldn't make sense. I had the qualifications. But I would have to finish the essays and submit them to the QEP before my mother and I left for Italy.

Incredible as it was, the trip to Milan was on. My mother hadn't budged on her decision to attend her friend Paola's fiftieth birthday party and she had offered to pay my way. Her only request was that we return to Maryland before November 24th, the one-year anniversary of my father's death. I was nervous about having sole responsibility for every aspect of the trip, but my sisters couldn't come with us to Milan because they had used up most of their vacations days.

In the end I told myself that, at this point, I had weathered so many unexpected twists and turns, I could handle any complications. In weighing the pros and cons, I saw the balance tipping in my favor. How could I say no to another trip to Italy?

13
You Can Do It

Eleven months since Dad's death.

To learn more about what I was getting myself into, I attended a Foreign Service information session at the School of Advanced International Studies at Johns Hopkins University. In the packed auditorium I saw several prospective applicants who appeared close to me in age. This reassured me, but when I heard the Foreign Service Officer Test being described as "a mile wide and an inch deep," I shrunk in my chair. The FSOT covered a daunting array of subjects: economics, principles of business and management, math and statistics, US government, US history, World history and more. *Oh my God*, I thought. *How can I possibly cram all that into my head?*

Apparently some test takers didn't study at all, but this was too much of a gamble, even for me. I had to pass the test—for my ego and future career. I ordered the official FSOT Study Guide, joined a study group, and bought books listed on a recommended reading list. I taped a world map to my bedroom wall and plastered my full-length bathroom mirror with the "Time Chart of World History." The study materials came with me to my mother's physical therapy sessions. Normally I used the time to buy groceries, but now I hunched over my books, highlighting key passages while Mom was being stretched and stimulated with electrodes.

Somewhere along the way I escorted my mother to her follow-up appointment with the neurologist. When we arrived at his office, the doctor plopped down at his desk and gave my mother a big grin.

"How are you feeling?" he said, as if she had just emerged from the healing river of the Ganges.

"Not bad," my mother said. "I'm trying."

I watched as the doctor reviewed her file. At this point I considered him minimally competent at best. If I hadn't been spinning so quickly through life, it would have occurred to me to yank my mother out of his office right then and there. But I wasn't connecting the dots, and I was completely out of my depth. More than anything, I was anxious to solve the riddle of my mother's oddly behaving brain. She kept losing things, and guessing what day of the week it was, tossing out days like darts at a board.

"We had you on the Namenda," the neurologist said, eyeing my mother. "Have you noticed any improvement with your memory?"

She turned to me, as if to say *how am I supposed to answer this?* Her uncertainty broke my heart.

"He's asking you, Mom, not me," I said softly.

After a moment, she said, "Well, no, I can't say that I have seen any improvement."

"Have you observed any changes?" the neurologist said, facing me.

"No." I wriggled a foot back and forth under my chair. He seemed to know something about my mother that he wasn't telling me.

"Now," he said to my mother, "I'm going to name three items that I want you to try and remember."

"Okay," my mother said, bracing herself, but agreeable.

"Watch, apple, table. Put those items aside in your mind. Now I want you to count backward from a hundred, subtracting in sevens."

"Let's see… ninety-three… eighty-six… seventy-nine… seventy-two…"

"Good. You can stop there. Can you name the current American president?"

"Clinton," said my mother. "No wait—Obama."

"How about the year?"

"2010," said my mother.

"Mmm-hmm. And the day of the week?"

"Monday."

It was Thursday, but the doctor didn't correct her.

"Now the three items I named earlier. Do you remember them?"

"Watch. Apple." Silence. My mother turned to me, furrowing her brow.

You can do it, I thought, glancing at the neurologist's desk, hoping my mother would get the hint. Hoping the neurologist was blind.

"Table," she said, smiling triumphantly.

Yes. I awaited his words of praise. But the neurologist wasn't impressed with my mother's performance. I guessed she did well enough, or he would have told me. Wouldn't he?

"I'm going to recommend that we switch medications," said the neurologist.

And with that I understood that he saw no improvement in my mother's memory and had decided it was time to try something else. *It's all trial and error,* I thought. I felt so dependent on the doctor's advice. But if there was any remedy for my mother, I wanted her to have it. I wanted her to be fixed.

"Axona is a powdered substance that you mix with water and take after a meal," said the neurologist, writing on his prescription pad. "Or, since it's a stable product, it can be mixed into just about anything. Oatmeal, pudding"—he tore off the paper and handed it to me—"some people even sprinkle it on ice cream. Let's see how this goes, and I'll see you in another seven weeks."

Thus began my mother's experiment with Axona.

Stable or unstable, my mother was disgusted by the medication. She tried making it work with milk, but it took her at least five minutes to drink the entire mixture. I watched from the sidelines, hoping she would get it down, even though I could see how much she hated it. I kept thinking *maybe this will help—maybe this is the miracle drug.* In between gulps, my mother would slam the cup down on the kitchen counter, and groan like a finalist in a hot dog eating contest.

"You can do it, Mom," I said. "Hang in there."

"Don't interrupt me," she replied.

She forged ahead, one swig at a time, determined to knock back the whole thing just to prove it could be done. Once my mother established that she was capable of consuming the whole glass, she changed her tactics. At first I was oblivious, but then I realized what she was up to, the giveaway being the extra amount of time she was spending at the kitchen sink. She stood with her back to me, drank half of the mixture, then poured the rest down the drain. I had to hand it to her. She was crafty all right.

"Mom," I said, "I doubt you'll see a benefit if you slice the dosage in half. If you can't stand the taste, just stop taking the medication."

She abandoned the Axona. It was the best solution for both of us.

THE FOREIGN SERVICE TEST wasn't until 10:30 a.m., but I was so wound up about it, I set two different alarms before going to bed—five minutes apart, in case one didn't go off—and printed out a map of the Howard University campus, where the exam was being given. These were nerve-calming precautions.

I arrived on campus at 9:30 a.m. and parked temporarily at a meter so that I could look at my map and locate the University Parking Center. I looked around to get my bearings, nervous enough about the test without having to acclimate myself to an unfamiliar setting. I scanned the brick buildings set between squares of grass, located the Parking Center, and hurried toward it through the chilly autumn air, intent on purchasing an all-day parking pass—another nerve-calming maneuver. I wasn't sure how long the exam would take, and the last thing I wanted to worry about was getting up in the middle of the exam to feed a meter.

I parked in a dingy lot across the street, darted between the cars, and found my way to the Student Resource Center back on campus. The Foreign Service exam was being given in the bowels of the building.

Arriving there, I handed over my Maryland driver's license, car keys, and wallet to an affable young black man, who stored my belongings in a locker.

"So you're going into the Foreign Service," he said, reaching for a point-and-shoot camera.

"Yes," I said, wondering if I could actually pull it off. For some reason, hearing a total stranger say it raised my doubts. "The public diplomacy track."

"Cool," said the young man.

He took my picture and presented me with a Non-Disclosure Agreement barring me from discussing the contents of the exam. I signed it and handed it back to him with a tight smile.

"In here," he said, leading me into a dimly lit room that resembled a stakeout location. "You can sit at any free computer. But once you're there, don't stray."

I glanced at the enclosed testing bays and the back of several heads. At one of the empty bays, I pulled out a chair and sat down. Above me was a filthy window and corroded iron bars on the other side. The street level sunlight was barely visible.

I moved the computer mouse, erasable tablet, and writing instrument from the right of the keyboard to the left side, to accommodate my nonuniversal hand. I told myself to relax, but the setup of the exam made it clear that I was up against a monster. Each of the four sections had to be completed within a precise time frame that ticked down on the computer screen as you worked through the sections. I started in on the English Expression section (sixty-five questions in fifty minutes). After completing it, I stood and stretched my hands high over my head.

"Don't wander," said the young man, edging in.

"Oh… sorry." I had moved less than a foot from my chair. I sat down again, rolling my head around a few times. Arching my back. I exhaled and clicked on to the next series of questions.

I completed the exam a little less than three hours later. My brain felt like a bowling ball. I collected my possessions and slogged up to the street level.

The air outside was crisp. Rays of autumn sun streaked through the trees. I soaked it up, relieved that the exam was over. But I wasn't sure about the argument I'd made on the thirty-minute timed essay. It was the last section and I had rushed through it, riding the rails energy-wise. But at least I had stuck to the recommended five-paragraph structure and refrained from creative flourishes, as recommended in the study guide. And I had reread the essay, checking the spelling and grammar before the clock ticked down to zero.

THE NEXT DAY I DROVE UP to New York City, released at last from my weeks of monomaniacal focus. Tasha had agreed to look after our mother during my Thursday-to-Sunday getaway. I couldn't wait to roam the streets of New York, unfettered. I planned to stay with friends from LA who now lived in

Hoboken, New Jersey, and drop in on my pal who worked at the edit facility in Soho. Then on Sunday, I would drive over to Maplewood, New Jersey to visit with a college friend and her partner. From there I'd drive back to Maryland.

Driving north on Interstate 95, I cranked up my electronic music like a teenager rocking out in her bedroom. I felt rebellious and free—from the exam and the strain of caring for my mother. It was the first time I'd traveled anywhere alone since leaving California.

Setting foot in lower Manhattan, I locked onto the rhythm of the city. It was cleaner and more barricaded than ever, but the frenetic energy was still there. October in New York was my favorite time of year. *New York is gorgeous in the fall*, I thought, smiling at the memory of my father's words in our last conversation. *Yes it is, Dad.*

Stepping into crosswalks, I waited the usual fraction of a second to let speeding cars pass, and then moved forward, whisking behind taillights—a cheap thrill that never got old. The tension left my body as I wove through the mass of pedestrians, invigorated by the nippy air and shafts of sunlight cutting through the skyscrapers. I rediscovered the lost art of walking quickly, and visited every gallery I could get into before closing time, inhaling art as if it might all disappear the next day. Riding the subways, slipping in and out of prewar buildings, and catching up with old friends, I gathered together the pieces of my left-behind past.

THOUGH I HAD WORKED OUT a viable plan for moving forward with my career, as the days passed, I began to feel apprehensive about the in-between part: writing the White

House volunteer book with my mother. I hadn't given it much thought until now, because the book was her idea, and my mother was so enthusiastic about it with that 4 a.m. note of hers. And I was preoccupied with another project: renovating my father's den. I plunged into the project, as a diversion while I awaited the results of my Foreign Service test, and because I needed to get past the sorrow I felt whenever I sat at my father's desk.

The classic executive was a midcentury modern gem with three drawers on either side of the seating area and a bookcase front. My father had been the original owner. But now my mother could barely look at it. Employing the same resolute tone as she had with my father's wardrobe, she told me to have the desk taken away. I decided to sell it on Craigslist. As I emptied the drawers, sorting through business cards wrapped in rubber bands, I imagined the relationships my father had formed with the names on the cards—travel agents, a computer technician, painter, electrician—and the restaurants where he and my mother had dined, catalogued in matchbooks he had saved. There were all kinds of batteries in the drawer, that only my father knew the use for, plus pens, pennies and little notes in Dad's sharp handwriting. It seemed blasphemous to throw things out, but I had no use for these objects. I put them in a clear, plastic shoe box, and tucked them in the closet.

In the bottom right drawer of the desk, I found a large, mustard-colored envelope. Inside, I discovered one of the first screenplays I'd ever written, bound with dull copper brads. I flipped through the age-softened pages, wincing at the clunky dialogue. My father must have known it was mediocre, but he kept it anyway. I let out a long breath and slipped the script back into its envelope, setting it aside. Weeping silent tears, I purged the remaining contents of the desk.

Once I sold the desk, I immersed myself in the happier aspects of the renovation, reveling in the satisfaction of creating something in stages. Laying down newspapers, scrubbing the walls, lining the ceiling with blue paint tape. *All very meticulous*, I kept thinking, *just like Dad.*

While the first coat of primer was drying, I went downstairs, tape recorder in hand.

"Mom?" I called out, figuring now was a good time to conduct an interview for the book.

I found my mother in the family room, lying down on the sofa.

"Hi," I said. "What do you say we do an interview for the book?"

"Not now," said my mother, sleepy-eyed. "I'm not up to it."

"Oh… well, how about in a couple of hours?"

"Sure," she said.

After the primer dried, I put on another coat and then returned to the family room.

"Are you ready?" I said, standing behind the couch, my mother on the other side. "Mom, please wake up," I said, disconcerted. "I need you."

"Can we do it later?" asked my mother.

"This is later."

"Then let's do it tomorrow," she said.

It went on like that for days. How would the book get written if my mother slept through the interviews? There had to be a way, but I couldn't think how, so I went back to something I could control: finishing off the den.

When the work was completed, I smiled at the salmon-colored walls. The entire room was infused with a Zen calm. The Spotlight Ebony desk I'd ordered from Crate & Barrel nicely offset the black-and-tan rug I bought from Ikea for fifteen dollars.

I was seized by an idea: instead of interviewing my mother, I would draft a proposal for the book. There was plenty of source material at hand, and I could do this on my own. I ran down to the basement and dug up my mother's FBI investigation from the late 1980s. Another file contained signed agreements, letters of thanks on White House stationery, and Scheduling Forms. The more I dug, the more material I found; I organized it chronologically, to create a timeline for the book.

Energized by my new plan of action, I began drafting the proposal, checking my e-mail relentlessly, strung out from the three-week wait for the results of my Foreign Service test.

AT THE END OF OCTOBER, while I was working on a sample chapter for the volunteer book, I clicked over to my Gmail account. My pulse quickened at the sight of an e-mail from ACT, the Foreign Service exam administrators. I leaned back in my chair, freaked out. Then I clicked on the e-mail and the embedded PDF file. Beneath the salutation were the words: "Congratulations! The scores you achieved on your Foreign Service Officer Test (FSOT) qualify you for the next step of the Foreign Service Officer selection process, which is your prompt submission of a personal narrative for review by the Qualifications Evaluation Panel (QEP)."

I leapt out of my chair—"Yes!"—fists raised, teary-eyed. It was the first piece of good news I'd had about my career since leaving California ten months ago.

I rushed downstairs to share the news with my mother. The family room was pitch dark, but I made out her arm as it shot up from the couch—my mother's way of signaling her location.

"I passed the Foreign Service exam," I said, turning on a light.

"Gee, that's terrific." My mother leaned upright.

"I'd say that calls for a drink."

"Absolutely," said my mother.

Everything was right in the world, for a precious few moments.

"Are we watching anything special on TV tonight?" my mother said.

"As a matter of fact we are. I rented a movie set in Milan, called *I Am Love*."

"Wonderful. So what happens next?"

"We have dinner and watch the movie."

"I mean with the Foreign Service thing," said my mother.

"Oh." I was opening a bottle of red wine, trembling with excitement. "I have to jump through the next hoop. Wow the review panel with my skills. And the essays are due before we go out of town. Ugh… I have to write five essays in ten days."

"You can do it," said my mother.

And naturally, I believed her.

14

The Deluge

Eleven-and-a-half months since Dad's death.

I SET TO WORK PLUMBING the depths of my experience, to describe, in thirteen-hundred characters or less, five situations where I used skills such as "the ability to plan and organize, set priorities, employ a systematic approach and allocate time and resources efficiently." *"I'm living it now,"* I thought. *Come to my house, and I'll show you.* But presumably the Qualifications Evaluation Panel meant nonfamily challenges, designed to showcase the professional skills I would bring to the Foreign Service.

In the midst of cobbling together my essays, walling myself off from all human interaction for hours at a time, I stopped long enough to take my mother to her third neurology appointment. My sense of futility had increased with each visit, but

I felt like I was caught up in an addiction I didn't know how to break.

When we arrived at the neurologist's office, I shared the news that my mother had stopped taking the Axona.

"That's too bad," he said, "but let's go ahead and see how you're doing with your powers of recollection. Can you name the current month?"

"October," said my mother.

"Okay, how about the date?"

"Um… the twenty-seventh."

My shoulders sagged. It was Thursday, November 4th.

"Can you name a recent big event?" said the neurologist.

My mother squinted. "That rally thing," she said.

She meant the Jon Stewart/Stephen Colbert "Rally to Restore Sanity" I had attended on the National Mall and described to her in detail.

"An event with national significance," he said. "It happened this past Tuesday."

I watched in dismay as my mother shook her head. The two of us had gone to the polls together, voting in the midterm elections at my old middle school. How could she forget physically getting into the car, driving there and walking into the school?

I guessed the neurologist was inured to all of this, because he kept on with a sort of cheery resignation, saying there wasn't much more he could do in terms of prescribing a medication.

"Exercise helps stimulate the brain," he said. "Are you exercising at all now?"

"No," said my mother. "I used to more often."

"What sort of exercise did you do?"

"Oh, what's the name of that thing," she said. "It begins with an 'R'."

"Mom has a recumbent bike in the basement," I said, upset and tired, wanting to leave.

"You need to get back on it," said the neurologist. "How do you spend your time during the day?"

My mother hesitated. "I write."

I knew this to be false, but was too distraught to speak.

"What was the last thing you wrote?" said the neurologist.

"A piece on the global economy," my mother said, "for the *National Herald*."

The neurologist beamed. "When did you write that?"

"Months ago," said my mother. "I guess it was a long time ago. I might write a piece on the rally that recently took place."

"Did you go to the rally?" said the neurologist.

"No."

"Oh." He paused. "Well, do you have clippings from the event?"

"Yes," said my mother.

That's not true, I thought, confused. I would have seen her clippings, if they existed.

"Why don't you tell the doctor about the book we're writing," I said.

Seconds passed, and then my mother said, "I can't recall the subject."

I lowered my head, close to tears. I realized my mother was mentally slipping away, and there was nothing I could do about it.

"We're… uh, we're writing a book about Mom's years working at the White House," I said, feeling a thousand miles away.

"That's terrific," said the neurologist, throwing up his hands, as if he'd finally struck gold. "That will sharpen your mind."

But now I wasn't sure the book would ever be completed. I could write the proposal on my own, but not the entire manuscript. For that I needed my mother.

I drove home with her in silence, troubled by her incorrect answers and the neurologist's carefree attitude. I realized he had never given us a definitive diagnosis.

A WEEK LATER, on the morning of our departure for Milan, I received an e-mail from Paola—our hostess and soon-to-be fifty-year-old—saying she was bedridden with the flu and wouldn't be able to pick us up at the airport as planned. With apologies, she asked that we take a taxi directly to our hotel. She had called the hotel and arranged for us to check in on the Friday of our arrival, instead of two days later, on the Sunday I had booked. Instead of our staying at her country home over the weekend, Paola's husband would take us out to the country on Saturday for a day trip, then bring us back to our hotel. I felt badly for Paola and hoped she felt better by her birthday. As for my mother and me, the abrupt change in plan was no big deal. Milan wasn't exactly a hardship post. As far as I knew.

THE RAIN BEGAN IN MUNICH, our connecting city to Milan. I observed the drizzle in passing, focused on getting to our next departure gate when we arrived at the Munich airport. I had purchased a collapsible wheelchair for the trip, and when we arrived at the airport, a travel aide emerged and took charge of my mother. I was groggy from the long flight and thankful for his assistance.

I followed the aide as he rolled my mother in her wheelchair through the mammoth glass and steel-pillared airport to the gate for our connecting flight. Having never traveled with anyone who needed assistance, I was astonished at the attention we received simply because we had brought the chair with us.

When it was time to board our connecting flight to Milan, a new travel aide materialized, clad in a rain slicker. He escorted us to a minibus reserved for the disabled and helped my mother board the bus. As he did this I thought, *that looks hard,* as if recognizing for the first time how demanding it was—on me—to care for my mother.

A little more than an hour after boarding our flight to Milan, we touched down under a wet sky at Malpensa airport. A chaotic jumble of activity ensued as I flagged down a random airport worker for help with my mother. I secured a luggage cart, retrieved our bags and followed a heavyset woman who pushed Mom out of the terminal in her wheelchair.

Though the rain had followed us from Munich to Milan, I barely registered the dampness, preoccupied with a pounding headache. I'd had too much to drink on the plane, celebrating the submission of my Foreign Service essays. I staggered out of the terminal with our luggage, watching as my mother was helped out of her wheelchair into a taxi van. The driver slotted the chair inside the van, met me with the luggage and quickly transferred it into the trunk as I dashed inside the taxi.

"Hotel Una, in Via Cusani," I said, when the driver got behind the wheel. "Prego."

AFTER CHECKING INTO the hotel, my mother and I squeezed into a two-person elevator and found the way to our junior suite. I had booked just the one room, on the theory that our trip was an extravagance and we didn't need to overdo it by staying in separate rooms. This turned out to be a major miscalculation. Unbeknownst to me, my mother was an extreme snorer. In fairness, I snored too. But not with her intensity. And our room faced the street, although I had requested a quiet room at the back of the hotel. I thought about calling the concierge to be relocated, but at that point switching rooms was a low priority. Between my agonizing headache, the time change and the disorienting effect of a new city, I could have slept through a mass demonstration.

I collapsed on one of the twin beds, next to my mother. Several hours later, I awoke to the sound of loud, scratchy breathing. I nudged my mother ever so slightly, and the room went quiet. I sat up, disoriented, but refreshed. My headache was gone. I went to the window, pulled aside the curtains. It was dark and wet outside. I couldn't make out any human activity on the cobblestone streets. The scene was so peaceful, I thought maybe we could avoid changing rooms after all. But then the air was pierced by a heaving sound. It was my mother revving up for the next round of snoring.

FIRST THING THE NEXT DAY, I spoke with the concierge about being moved into separate rooms for our remaining eight nights, preferably on a quiet side of the hotel. The concierge explained that the hotel was heavily booked, but he would see what he could do. A few minutes later, Paola's husband

Beppe arrived in the lobby to pick up my mother and me for our day in the country.

"Everything is okay with the room?" he inquired, hugging me, gregarious as ever.

"It's not what we asked for," I said. "But…"

"I'll see," said Beppe, heading straight to the front desk.

I overheard him speaking emphatically in Italian to the concierge. It seemed far more effective than anything I might achieve as an English-speaking American. I crossed my fingers.

We slipped out into the rain, into Beppe's SUV parked at the curb. His nineteen-year-old daughter Carola greeted us from inside the car. She was warm and full of energy, just like her father. Off to the country we went.

The house in Azzate was set back on a deep lawn that overlooked a valley. By the time we arrived there, the rain had stopped, but the misty air compounded my sense of dislocation, and as I took in the view, sluggish from the trip, I wondered when we would see Paola. She was at the center of our plans, but absent thus far.

We all ambled into the house, and Beppe made a fire before breaking out the wine, while Carola heated a creamy pasta and meat casserole prepared in advance by Paola. As we ate and talked about our various plans for the coming week, my mother mostly kept quiet, methodically working through her meal. I guessed she was still jet-lagged.

"How is Helen doing?" Beppe asked me afterward.

We were working off our heavy lunch, strolling in a nearby grove, while Mom took a nap.

"I wish I knew," I said. "She's forgetful and has trouble speaking sometimes. But her neurologist doesn't have any answers. Or if he does, he's not sharing them." I paused. "She sleeps a lot. Maybe that's why her brain is so fuzzy."

"Hmm... is it a year since Peter died?"

"Not yet," I said. "The anniversary is on the twenty-fourth."

I felt out of sorts, barely able to recall the events of a year ago. They were obscured by all the emotions I'd experienced since then, plus my ongoing concerns about how much time my mother spent in bed. Under the colorless sky, I felt the weight of responsibility for her well-being pressing down on my shoulders. I hoped the weather improved. It was always easier for me to deal with adversity in the sunshine.

BEFORE LEAVING THE US I had sent Paola an e-mail urging her to see *I Am Love*, the movie set in Milan that my mother and I had seen. I raved about the mansion where much of the action took place. To my surprise, Paola did some research and learned that the mansion, the Villa Necchi Campiglio, was open to the general public. She was still on antibiotics and couldn't leave her house, but she had arranged for Beppe to take us there for a tour.

On the designated day, it rained intermittently, but the tour of the Villa put a sparkle in the air. The museum-like mansion had been built in the early 1930s for a wealthy industrial family; it was a ravishing monument to excess, with immaculate grounds draped in lush foliage. Angled across from the main entrance was a long, rectangular pool, framed with yellow and white flowers. I imagined it brilliantly lit under a black sky, and mentally replayed the dramatic night scene between Tilda Swinton's character and her son in the film, *I Am Love*.

I felt transported. Having viewed the movie from our family room couch, I was now inside the screen. But I was disheartened by my mother's slow progress through the mansion, and kept thinking, *I should have brought the wheelchair.* Halfway through the tour, she had to sit down. And she was silent most of the time we were out, as she had been in the country. In the car, and later at lunch in the nearby café, I realized I was carrying the conversation for both of us. Was my mother still jet-lagged? Where was her mind?

WHEN WE RETURNED TO the hotel, I swiftly packed up our luggage, rejoicing at the latest development: the concierge had found us separate rooms on different floors. It was only for two nights, because the hotel was booked for the rest of our stay, but when I got into my room, I threw myself on the bed, liberated by the solitude.

Later that night, on our way out to dinner, I approached the front desk while my mother wandered off in the direction of the hotel dining room.

"Is there any way we can remain in our suites?" I said, summoning my most forlorn expression.

The concierge shook his head. "The best I can do is let you know if there are cancellations."

"All right. I'll check back with you."

I went in search of my mother, and found her at the bar, nibbling on some pistachios.

"Not much chance of keeping our rooms," I said. "But I'll ask again."

She seemed oblivious to my words, cracking her nuts, popping the green dots in her mouth.

"You should pitch those," I said, as we moved toward the hotel exit. "It's raining and dark outside. Walking and shelling pistachios at the same time is not a good idea."

"I'll be fine," said my mother.

I exhaled, frustrated, as she wrapped an arm through mine. We set out into the rain with our umbrella, crossing over streetcar tracks and the cobblestone road.

"Watch where you're going," I said, seeing my mother was focused on her pistachios.

We curled left onto Via Ponte Vetero, hugging the wall as we crept along the narrow sidewalk, elevated about six inches from the main road. I should have been on my mother's right side, so she could walk along the wall instead of the curb, but I was so used to hooking onto her left side, I did it now automatically.

All of a sudden I felt a sharp pull on my right arm.

"Oh!" my mother cried—and in an instant I saw her slip and fall headlong into the road.

"Mom!" I dropped the umbrella and rushed into the road. "Oh my God—grab onto me!"

In a horrific flash I saw the rain pelting down on her crumpled body as a car moved toward us. *It's moving slowly*, I thought, shaking. *We can make it to the sidewalk.*

My mother grabbed onto me for dear life as I helped her to the sidewalk using both arms.

"My rings—I lost my diamond rings!" she said.

"Stay there!" I said. "Don't move."

My eyes shot back to the road, at the rainwater rippling in and around the crevices of the cobblestones—trickling over a bump of glass. It was my mother's diamond nugget, shimmering under the streetlight where the sidewalk met the road. Alongside it was her diamond-encrusted band. I lurched into the road and scooped up both rings just before I saw the lights of an oncoming car. I rushed back to the sidewalk and thrust the rings in my mother's hands.

"Here," I said, furious. "Are you happy now? You had your pistachios and you almost got us both killed. Jesus Christ—don't ever do that again. You scared the hell out of me!"

My mother nodded, shaken in a way I hadn't seen since my father's death. It seemed like the first time she realized her actions could affect someone else.

I held onto her tightly as we made our way to a randomly chosen restaurant. Inside, the maitre' d led us past the bar and up two steps, to a table next to a window.

"Thank you," I said, collecting myself.

My mother and I sat across from each other. As I reached for my glass of water, I thumped it down, seeing a patch of red on her right forearm.

"Mom, you're bleeding."

She pulled up her sleeve, stared at the bloody, six-inch scrape on her arm.

I ran to the bathroom and ripped some paper towels out of the dispenser, wiping my eyes as I ran the water over the paper towels. I stood there a moment, covering my mouth, depressed and frantic at the same time. I went back to the table.

"Here," I said, handing my mother the moist towels.

As soon as the waiter arrived, I ordered us each a glass of red wine.

IN THE MORNING, after a late breakfast in the hotel restaurant, my mother went back to her room to read and sleep, while I fetched an umbrella and headed outside. It was raining for the fourth day in a row, but I was determined to do some exploring, even if it felt like I wasn't in Milan. In fact I wasn't exactly sure where I was. The rain blurred everything together, and the circular streets messed with my sense of direction. I struck out on a road I was familiar with, eager to go back to Fabriano, a paper store we had briefly visited on the weekend.

Wandering inside the store, I marveled at the beautifully displayed desk accessories arranged in modular white cubbyholes. The organizational aspect of everything seemed to set my mind right. I spent more than an hour in the store, studying the craftsmanship of leather, zippered pencil cases and metallic mechanical pencils. In the end I bought a green wooden pencil, a squat orange pen and a red leather note holder. I watched with admiration as each item was carefully wrapped in tissue paper and tucked into a thick paper bag closed with a red strip of tape.

From there I went into a vintage clothing store and also a couple of shoe stores. I didn't buy anything. I didn't need anything. I just enjoyed being on my own, moving at a nimble pace.

I returned to the hotel and checked in on my mother. When she opened the door I saw her room was dark as night.

"What time is it?" said my mother, barefoot and groggy, wearing a thick white bathrobe.

"Four o'clock," I said, momentarily confused by her appearance.

"I'm going back to bed," said my mother.

"Oh… okay. Remember we have to be at Paola and Beppe's at seven for dinner. I'll come back for you at six-fifteen."

"I'll be ready" my mother said.

I went back to my room, crashed for an hour, and then showered and dressed for the evening. At six-fifteen, I knocked on my mother's door. She didn't answer. I knocked again.

My mother opened the door, appearing in a slit of darkness. She was still in her bathrobe, disheveled and barefoot.

"Why aren't you dressed?" I said, pushing into the room.

I fumbled for a light switch, finding one above the night table. The lamp illuminated, I saw my mother lying down again.

"Mom, please don't go back to bed," I said, my throat tightening.

"I'll get up in ten minutes."

I knew she hadn't taken a bath, which meant we wouldn't leave for dinner until seven at the earliest. In any case we would definitely be late, and probably by more than fifteen minutes.

"Come on, Mom," I begged. "It takes time for you to get ready, and we need to leave soon." She didn't move or say anything. "What's wrong? Are you sick? Do you want to stay in?"

"No," she moaned. "Just give me ten minutes."

"We're going to be late," I said, moving toward the bathroom. "Come on. I'll fill the tub with water and you can take a quick bath."

Inside the bathroom, I saw her rack of pills on the marble countertop. The slot for today was full. My mother had forgotten to take her medications. I glanced at my watch. It was six twenty-five.

I opened the spigots on the bathtub, went back to the sink, filled a glass with tap water, and returned to the bedroom with the pill dispenser. My mother was sitting on the edge of the bed, massaging her eyes. I held up the glass of water and her opened rack of pills.

"Take these," I said.

"Put them on the night table."

Startled into submission, I set down the pills and watched my mother lumber toward the bathroom. "I'll be ready in ten minutes," she said.

I wanted to believe her. I sat in a club chair, staring at the closed bathroom door. In a moment I heard the running tub water shut off. I glanced at the stockings draped over an armchair, the scrambled bed sheets, and then the bathroom door. It was 6:40 p.m.

"How are you doing in there?" I called out.

Silence. At 6:45 p.m. my mother came out of the bathroom, lipstick first, her bright red mouth dotting the shadowy room. Without a word she pulled the hosiery off the armchair and sat on the edge of the bed in her bathrobe, opening it slightly to pull on her stockings.

"What are you going to wear?" I said.

"That."

My mother flung an arm in the direction of a print dress hanging over the closet door. It was covered in clear plastic from the dry cleaner's. I removed the plastic and held up the dress.

She reviewed it and said, "The other one, I think."

"What's wrong with this one?"

"I don't want to wear it," my mother said, annoyed. "The one behind it is better."

I rewrapped the dress and hung it on the closet door. By then my mother had finished putting on her stockings and was heading back into the bathroom. Confused, I looked at my watch. It was 7:00 p.m., the time of our dinner.

In a moment my mother came out of the bathroom, fingering a pair of clip-on earrings.

"What are you doing?" I said. "We have to go!"

"Just calm down," she said, replacing her pearl earrings with the clip-ons.

"I'm being as calm as possible," I said, "considering how late we are."

"Well, it will all be over in a week," said my mother.

Hard and cold. Like the voice I'd heard months ago, after the literary luncheon. Only now I was less forgiving. Nearly a year had passed since my father's death, and my tiny ball of stress had swollen into a boulder-sized tumor.

"That is so unfair," I said. "You had all day to get ready, and now you're giving *me* a hard time? Give me a fucking break. You know, you're always saying 'self-pity is the worst.' But right now you're so full of self-pity you can't even imagine someone else feeling pain. You're upset because you lost your husband. Well, guess what? I lost a father. I *miss* my father! This is hard for me, too! Can you understand that?"

I was trembling and wanted to cry, but I didn't want to show up for dinner looking as if I'd been bawling all night.

My mother didn't say a word. She just climbed into her shift, jostled it over her hips and poked her arms through the sleeves. Then she turned around, her back facing me.

"Can you zip me up, please?"

It wasn't a request. I zipped her up, cowed by her composure.

And then it hit me. I realized my mother didn't want to be here. She had vacationed in Milan with my father, and her memories of the city were with him. I wasn't the person she wanted to be with. I wasn't Dad. I wasn't even her daughter. I was a dresser. A chauffeur. An organizer who made things happen. I felt light-headed, as if I were about to collapse.

THE ARGUMENT HAD so undone me that I'd forgotten to call Paola to let her know we were running late. But when we arrived at seven thirty, she shrugged it off. I remembered we were in Europe. Half an hour wasn't *late*. Paola showed us around the large apartment, apparently unaware of my frayed nerves. Her ongoing illness had kept us from seeing her until now, but she was optimistic about recovering by Friday, when we would celebrate her birthday.

My mother put on quite a show for her Italian friends, rising to the occasion in a truly masterful way. Between her expert ability to keep up appearances, and my determination to get through the evening, I was sure our hosts thought the rain was our only challenge in Milan.

LATER, BACK AT THE HOTEL, I escorted my mother to her room and gave her a perfunctory kiss goodnight before doubling back to the elevator. My room was one flight up. When I arrived there, I fell back onto the bed and stared at the ceiling, replaying the argument from earlier in the evening.

In a moment my cheeks felt flush, my chest expanding and contracting. Tears came into my eyes. I felt feverish and sweaty. I grabbed the global cell phone off the nightstand and called Zoë.

As soon as she answered the phone I began sobbing through my words. I told her about our mother's fall in the rain and how terrifying it was to see her out flat in the road. About the lost diamond rings, the pills our mother wasn't taking and her incessant sleeping. The room changes. The rain. The argument this evening. How our mother had said *it will all be over in a week*. As if our costly trip to one of the most beautiful cities in the world was just a time-filler.

"I can't do this anymore," I said, hugging myself, rocking on the edge of the bed.

"I'm sorry," said Zoë. "I know it's hard for both of you."

"But I'm doing everything. It's too much. I need help. A nursing aide or something—please." I held the phone tight against my ear.

"I'll do some research tonight," said Zoë, "and tell Tasha to, also. We'll get you some help."

"Please."

"Do you have access to the Internet there?" said Zoë.

"I… I think I saw a computer in the lobby, but I haven't used it."

"I'll send you an e-mail update. Or we can talk about it when you get back."

"I can wait until then," I said. "Just do the research. Thank you."

You're getting help, I kept telling myself. *Help is on the way.*

IN THE MEANTIME, in Milan, my mother and I settled into a détente. The rain continued as we moved into our third and final accommodation at the Hotel Una Cusani. I felt like a weary carnival worker, splashing from one town to the next. The days rained on; I meandered the streets mostly alone, branching out to the shops around the corner. At times I prodded my mother out of bed to have her come with me, but taking in the sights with her wasn't exactly uplifting. My mother seemed detached from her surroundings, as if it were all old hat. But there was one exception: the night we went to the opera.

Paola had managed to secure two tickets for my mother and me to see a production of *Carmen* at the infamous Teatro alla Scala. I had only been to one opera performance in my life—*Madame Butterfly* at Lincoln Center—but opera was one of my father's great passions, so I thought if anything would patch over the nasty argument I'd had with my mother, it would be this performance, where our memories of Dad would bind us together.

Curtain time was 8 p.m. I wasn't about to risk a repeat performance of our Monday night throw down, so I made sure my mother was awake and ready to go at 7 p.m., and called a taxi to take us to La Scala, even though it was within walking distance of the hotel. It was just as well, because of course it was raining.

Inside the round opera house, I rolled my head back, mouth agape at the scarlet curtain draped across the stage and spectacular chandelier hanging from the white-domed ceiling. The main floor, or *platea*, was filled with rows of red upholstered seats. Box seats trimmed in gold were roped around the theatre. I had heard that the highest section, the *loggione*, was where the most critical audience members sat—the opera fanatics who knew every bar of the score and threw programs at the stage if a performance fell flat. By contrast, the audience in the *platea* applauded politely no matter what the level of performance. My mother and I sat in this section, eight rows from the stage. I was so excited to be there I would have applauded a chimpanzee.

It seemed we were destined to see *Carmen*. The tragic-comedy about a soldier who falls in love with a hot-blooded gypsy was the perfect antidote for my aching heart, and my mother's, too, I suspected. Throughout the lively presentation I thought of my father. I knew he was with us in spirit. As the performers took their bows, I stood up with everyone and shouted "Bravissimo!"

Dizzy with excitement, I emerged from the theater with my mother. It was still drizzling, and there were no cabs in sight, but I knew the way back to the hotel well enough to guide us there on foot. We locked arms, and pitched into the cold, heads under the umbrella.

"That was good," said my mother.

"Pure magic," I said.

"We have a good time together." My mother paused. "Most of the time."

I had to laugh.

OUR ITALIAN FRIENDS retrieved us from the hotel for Paola's fiftieth birthday celebration. The reason for our trans-Atlantic journey had finally come to pass. But the birthday wasn't our only cause for celebration. That day the sun had made a brief appearance, and Paola had recovered enough from her illness to stroll the city with my mother. While the two of them went shopping, I had lunch with a friend of Zoë's who lives in Milan. It was the first and last time during our nine-day trip that my mother spent any daylight hours with Paola.

I thought about this when I saw how Paola doted on my mother at the birthday party. Wistful for what might have been, I was certain the two of them spending more time together would have eased the tension between my mother and me. But at least we had made it through the week without having any more blow-ups.

The restaurant where the party was held had a rough exterior that belied its chic, minimalist interior. We trickled inside, winding through tables draped in white and sturdy black chairs set on hardwood floors. Paola introduced us to the chef, and led us to an alcove enclosed by floor-to-ceiling glass. Overhead, a fat copper heating tube hung from the wood ceiling. It was an intimate space, with two of the six tables reserved for her dinner party.

I was still on a high from our night at La Scala, and my mother seemed to be, too, although she was smiling more than talking. During dessert, I brought Paola up to speed on my mother's overall health and shared my concerns about her forgetfulness.

"She is a bit more engaged," said Paola, surreptitiously eyeing my mother.

"Since you saw her in Tuscany."

"Yes, I think so."

"Hmm."

I hadn't noticed, maybe because I was so preoccupied with getting my mother out of bed every day. But I also knew that among friends, she often rose to the occasion.

It was a lively celebration, but I was anxious to return home, worn out from the constant rain and the strain of caring for my mother.

Two days later, we checked out of the Hotel Una Cusani at the break of dawn, speeding through the rain to Malpensa airport. I felt like an evacuee. The deluge had lasted eight days.

As our Frankfurt-bound jet rose through the clouds and emerged onto a blanket of bright blue sky, I nudged my mother, pointing at the beams of yellow light beyond our window.

"Mom, look—sunshine."

She glanced up from her orange juice. "How about that."

WHEN WE LANDED AT Dulles airport, I felt like I needed a vacation from my vacation. The trip had been much more demanding than I had anticipated, both emotionally and physically. Fittingly, I had picked up a cold on the way back, and sneezed throughout the flight from Germany to DC.

After deplaning at Dulles, I rolled my mother in her wheelchair, woozy and sniffling my way through the slowly snaking Customs line. Clearing the checkpoint, I steered the chair through the exit doors, overcome with relief at the sight of Tasha on the other side. I shot up an arm and heaved the chair forward.

Back at the house, Tasha sat with us at the kitchen table as we recapped our adventures in Milan—minus the twin disasters of my mother's plunge into the street and our Monday night throwdown. But when my mother went upstairs, I gave my sister the rest of the story.

"The whole trip was like a one-stop shop for everything that could go wrong," I said.

"Oh, gosh," said Tasha.

"I mean, there were some bright spots, and I did agree to go, but I wouldn't do it again. And I definitely need help with Mom."

"Okay," said Tasha, nodding blankly.

I wasn't sure whether she understood the extent of my burden. But we agreed to have a family meeting when Zoë arrived for Thanksgiving, to discuss bringing in a home health aide for a few hours each week.

After Tasha left, I stole a few moments of solitude, sifting through the mail. It was mostly magazines and junk mail addressed to my father, despite his being dead for nearly a year. I ached at the sight of his name. I had called and sent e-mails asking for it to be removed from countless mailing lists, but new vendors kept cropping up like a Whack-A-Mole, eager to pitch my father some service even as he lay in his grave. I gathered up the latest batch, turned the pile over, and set it aside. As I was powering up my laptop, my mother came into the kitchen.

"I could really go for a bowl of *avgolemono* soup," she said.

"How would that happen?" I said, straining for a playful tone.

The Greek restaurant we ordered the egg-and-lemon soup from was a ten-minute drive from our house. As we were outside the delivery radius and my mother no longer drove, there was only one way the soup would get to our house.

"We could go out," said my mother, meaning *you could go out and get it for me.*

"Mom, I'm not going out," I said. "Why don't you warm up some roasted red pepper soup?"

"Okay," she said.

My mother found the soup in the cupboard and emptied the entire quart-size box into a pot on the stove. After heating it up, she ladled a third of it into a bowl, sat down with it at the kitchen table, and read the *New York Times.*

"Is there anything we can watch on TV tonight?"

I glanced at my watch. "Mom, it's one thirty in the morning, Italy time."

"I'm not tired," she said.

Of course not, I thought. *Because you didn't schlepp both of us across the ocean.*

"Well, I am," I said. "I'm checking my e-mails and going straight to bed."

"That's fine," said my mother, going back to the *Times.*

I studied the barrage of e-mails between my sisters, written while I was in Italy. I hadn't logged onto the hotel computer, and was seeing the e-mails for the first time. The one that jumped out at me was a message Tasha had sent in reference to an organization called Capital City Nurses: "Jana, when you return we can discuss how many hours per day/week would be good for you."

Yes, I thought, feeling lighter.

"I'm going to bed," said my mother, stepping away from the table.

"Uh… okay." I was thinking about how many home health aide hours *would be good* for me.

My mother placed her soup bowl in the sink, and left the kitchen.

Glancing around the room, I had a sense of déjà vu. Newspapers, magazines, opened boxes, and plastic bags were scattered everywhere. Shoes that my mother had bought in Italy were planted on the countertop. The unused portion of her soup was in the pot on the stove, the ladle inside. My head throbbed as I thought about my options. I wouldn't be able to fall asleep knowing the soup was congealing overnight on the stove. And I had no desire to confront a kitchen in disarray tomorrow morning. I shut off the computer, got up and tidied the kitchen.

THE NEXT MORNING, when I saw my mother at breakfast, it occurred to me that she hadn't taken a bath in three days—a troubling thought, especially given that the bath had taken place in another country.

"Why don't you take a bubble bath after breakfast?" I said.

"I don't have the energy," said my mother.

"Let me run the bath for you."

"No thanks," said my mother.

I lowered my head, depressed by her apparent lack of concern for her hygiene.

Later, in the den, I struggled with my draft proposal for the White House volunteer book, preoccupied with my mother's dull mood. And then, when I saw her return to her bedroom and close the door behind her, I was overcome with sadness. My mother was going back to bed—barricading herself from the world. I told myself her woes were amplified because we were coming up on the one-year anniversary of my father's death, on November 24.

"I just want to get past it," my mother kept saying, whenever the topic came up.

And it came up often now, because autumn was here and Thanksgiving was close at hand. This holiday that coincided with my father's death had been redefined in our family.

In my own mind, November 24 couldn't come soon enough. I don't know what I thought would change, in terms of my mother's condition, but I knew she would remain in her funk until the day passed. I didn't want to think about how it would affect me if her funk persisted after that.

15

A Better Place

One-Year Anniversary of Dad's death.

I DROVE THROUGH THE black iron gates of the cemetery, fingers cold on the wheel of my mother's Mercedes. The sky was leaden, and the sprawling grounds of the Gate of Heaven Cemetery were empty, but for the odd maintenance worker gathering up bits of windswept ribbon and vine. At the spread of lawn before me, I turned right and followed the road to a grassy roundabout near my father's gravesite. I parked and shut off the engine.

"Are you ready?" I asked my mother, shivering with apprehension.

She nodded, rocking ever so slightly in the passenger seat. "I'll get the flowers."

I retrieved the irises from the back seat and helped my mother out of the car.

"I think it's up here," I said, as we navigated the lawn pocked with headstones.

My father's grave had been unmarked for a year. On past visits—alone, because my mother couldn't bring herself to come—I was sure I sat on the wrong patch of dirt at least twice and conversed with someone who wasn't my father. But now, as I moved farther up the hill, I jerked back at the sight of our family name spelled out in large capital letters:

+ PANARITES +

There it is, I thought, fixated on the bronze plaque. My father's name and the years.

His beginning and his end: 1930–2009.

I let out a deep breath. We were at my father's end. The real end. Not the slow-burn ending of the wake and the funeral, or the finale of his burial on November 28. Not the ending relived with every *first* without Dad. This was the sealed-shut ending of a marker in the earth, confirming what I knew and must now accept: *He is here and you are there and that is how it must be.*

Etched into the plaque's upper left corner were my father's first and middle names: PETER ERNEST. I stared at the names, then looked at my mother's in the opposite corner: HELEN PAPSON, Papson being her maiden name, shortened from Pappadopoulos. Gazing at her name on the plaque, as my mother stood next to me, I realized she was straddling two worlds: the one above the earth and the one below ground. "Any time you're ready!" the one below seemed to say.

I felt my insides tighten. *She had to have that combination plaque*, I thought, remembering the day in mid-May when my mother and I placed the order—a bonding experience like no other, in the cemetery office, where slabs of bronze were propped up on the floor like sample kitchen countertops. My mother had decided on the combination plaque so that she and my father could be united on the marker as they had been in life. A design was selected, a font chosen. Forms were filled out and a check handed over. Four months later, the plaque was fixed to the earth. We were viewing it today for the very first time.

I bent at the knees and unscrewed the in-ground vase.

"I'll get some water," I said, moving to a knee-high, green spigot. I returned a few moments later with the water-filled vase and secured it to my father's plaque. Unwrapping the irises, I arranged the stems in the urn, the spray of purple popping brightly against the bronze plaque.

"There," I said. "Doesn't that look nice?"

My mother nodded, lips pressed together.

I faced the grave, imagining my father lying parallel to the earth in his navy blue Brooks Brothers suit and soft yellow tie. Dead in his box, shrunken to the bone.

"We took off his glasses, didn't we?" said my mother.

"Yes," I said, and then to pre-empt the inevitable next question, I added, "There was a drawer." Meaning the cubbyhole inside the casket where we'd placed my father's eyeglasses.

But when someone goes to *a better place*, why does he need eyeglasses? Isn't everything in focus in that *better place*?

The sight of my mother's name on the marker unnerved me, but there was one saving grace. There was just one year next to her name: 1929, the year of her birth. Still, there *was* that blank space next to the year, waiting to be filled in. And it would be filled in. I knew that now. One day my mother would lay here next to my father, and the story of their lives would then be complete.

I put an arm around my mother, defying the blank space. Shielding her from it. Shielding me. *Not yet*, I thought. *Please, not soon. No bracketed years.*

My mother closed her eyes in prayer, her tinted eyeglasses hiding the wetness in her eyes. Her pumpkin-colored car coat, giant-checked Burberry scarf, and black wool gloves with the white buttons were an odd reminder that—despite the hole in her heart—her sense of style had remained intact for an entire year. I looked away, realizing that since my father's death, this was the only thing about my mother that had remained intact. Her heart was in tatters, her memory fading away. A year after my father's death, she was still floating through life, sometimes engaged, but most often not, sometimes vertical, but mostly horizontal (preferably in bed, but a couch would do). *The escape artist*, my mother called herself, aware of her ongoing preference for shutting out the world, because a world without my father wasn't worth joining.

The longer I stood over my father's grave, the more I realized how little grieving I had done for the man beneath my feet. I realized that while my mother had spent the last year mourning him, I had spent most of it mourning her. During the past year my mother and I had cried together and argued, and occasionally laughed with each other. At times I had felt profoundly close to her, but mostly I felt further away from her than the literally thousands of miles we traveled together.

Our separation had begun on the night of my father's death, and continued with each passing hour, from the wake to the funeral, and every day after that. *The funeral*, I thought, remembering how my mother had slipped the laminated prayer card into my father's casket. The one with the words *Miss Me But Let Me Go* written on the back.

I glanced at the sky, repeating the words in my mind. *Miss Me But Let Me Go.*

Startled, I realized the words were written for my father, but could be applied to my mother. For so much of the past year, I had been waiting for that fearless bundle of energy who raised me to resurface. I missed that mother dearly. But now I realized that I needed to let go of her and accept that she wasn't coming back. She was lost to my father and to the memories they had formed together. We were satellites in their orbit, my sisters and me. They belonged to each other before they belonged to us.

I realized I had fallen into a trap, unknowingly buying into the idea that grief can be regulated. I had always been good at managing time, setting goals and meeting deadlines. I had created so many finite endings. But I failed to understand that some things never end. Standing there next to my mother, I realized that her longing for my father would never come to an end.

I felt overwhelmed, as if I finally understood my mother as a whole person—and learned something new about myself: that I could accept her condition no matter where it led or how it affected my future. But I wanted to believe that my mother could hold onto her memories of my father without being debilitated by them for the rest of her life. I didn't know how long it would take for her to get to that point. The only thing I knew for sure was that we would both be better off if I left the timetable to her.

16

The Escape Hatch

"I want to put up a Christmas tree," I said at breakfast one morning. Now that we were past the one-year anniversary of my father's death, I felt emboldened to make some changes.

"I'd rather not," said my mother.

"Too bad. I'm making an executive decision. We didn't have a tree last year, and I'm tired of all the gloom and doom in this house."

"No," my mother said, whining. "I don't want you dragging a tree through the back door with all those pine needles scattered everywhere."

"Who said anything about dragging a tree through the back door? I'm ordering an artificial tree from Home Depot."

"But… how can you do that?" said my mother.

"Mom, you can order anything online."

"Fine," she said. "Do what you want."

I went online and ordered the artificial tree with preinstalled white lights. It arrived a week later, in a cardboard box the size of a small couch. We had never had a fake tree in our house, but after setting it up and triggering the lights, I was a convert. The purist in me preferred a real one, but the Hollywood applauded the fake.

"Gosh, that is nice," said my mother, marveling at the Downswept Douglas.

"And look," I said, waving a hand across the floor. "No pine needles."

I sat down at the piano, and played it for the first time in a year, poking my way around a jazzed-up version of *Silent Night*.

"That's so wonderful to hear," said my mother, sitting down next to me. "It's been so long since you played."

"Too long." I felt her putting her head on my shoulder. "You know how much I love you, right?" I said, choking back my tears.

"I do," said my mother, wiping her eyes. "It goes both ways."

When I went to bed that night, I saw the sheets were folded back.

I PUSHED FOR more changes.

"Yes," I said, nodding repeatedly when her doctor suggested my mother start seeing a psychologist. "That's a great idea."

"I'll give you a list of therapists who take Medicare," said Dr. Post.

"Okay," said my mother, in a small voice. "If you think I should go, I will."

"I do," said the doctor. "It's good to talk about your feelings."

It took you a year to tell her that? I thought. But I bit my tongue. We were going in the right direction, and that was all that mattered.

"It's been a year since your husband died," Dr. Post said to my mother. "And I'm concerned that you're not engaging more with life."

My mother gave me a despondent look. In fact she was sleeping now more than ever.

"We were going to write a book together," I said. "But… I'm not sure that's going to happen."

I knew I couldn't write the White House volunteer book on my own, and it seemed unlikely my mother would be awake long enough for me to conduct any useful interviews. I remembered the pact I'd made with myself, to let her go at her own pace. But if we weren't going to write the book, what would I do during the months before I entered the Foreign Service?

"You should get involved in some sort of project," said Dr. Post, eyeing my mother.

"I'll try," she said.

"And I'll make that therapy appointment," I said.

When we got home, I googled one of the therapists on the list Dr. Post had given me, a woman whose practice was focused on geriatric and grief-related issues. Her name sounded Danish. *I like the Danes*, I thought. I called and left her a message.

That same afternoon, I was pulling into the parking lot at Giant Foods when my BlackBerry rang.

"Hello?"

"Uh, hi. I'm returning a call from… is it Jana?"

It was the therapist. "Yes, that's me," I said. "Thank you for returning my call. I got your name from Dr. Rosalyn Post, my mother's primary care physician. She suggested Mom get some counseling. I'm calling on her behalf."

"Why do you think she needs counseling?" said the therapist.

I shut off my car engine, thinking *where do I begin?* "I guess the best way to answer that is to explain how active my mother was when my father was alive, and how lethargic she is now."

I felt a spiraling anxiety, cataloguing my mother's behavior over the past year—garbled thoughts spilling out of my mouth like a machine gun spitting bullets. Thankfully, the therapist didn't hang up on me. When I finished my spiel, I waited for her response. And waited.

"I... I'm sorry, but I'm not taking any new clients," she said.

"Please...?"

"Well... I would be willing to meet with your mother for a consultation, but I can't commit to anything beyond that."

"Thank you," I said. "Thank you so much." I made the appointment for next week, jotting it down on a scrap of paper found in the glove compartment.

AN INTAKE SPECIALIST from Capital City Nurses came to our house. We'd had our family meeting and everyone was on board with my getting help, including my mother.

"Mostly we need someone to take Mom to her physical therapy appointments," I said to the intake specialist, "and help her run a bath, change her sheets, that sort of thing. Oh—and hang out with her when she's using the exercise bike in the basement."

"How about preparing meals?" she said, scribbling away.

I watched with excitement. "Sure. Setting up Mom's breakfast would be great."

"I'm agreeable to that," said my mother.

"We have a four-hour per day minimum," said the woman.

"Why don't we start with two days per week," I said. "Is that okay, Mom?"

She nodded. "Sure. I'm ready for it."

The intake specialist packed up her notebook. She told us a coordinator would review her assessment and call with a proposed candidate for the job.

THE FOLLOWING MONDAY was my mother's consultation with the psychologist. I had planned to take her, but as the weekend approached I felt feverish, so Tasha took her instead.

When they returned to the house after the session, my mother told me she felt at ease with the therapist and saw the benefit of going back. It turned out the therapist, named Joan, could fit my mother into her schedule after all. She would see Mom every Monday. I was elated.

"Mom really likes her," said Tasha, after our mother went to lie down.

"That's great," I said. "And the new caregiver can drive her to the appointments."

"Oh, no. She doesn't want anyone coming to the house."

"What?" I stiffened.

"I sat in on part of the session," said my sister, "and when the subject came up, Joan asked Mom how she felt about it and she shook her head and said no."

"But that's not what we agreed to."

Tasha shrugged. "She doesn't want it."

"But I need help. We already had an intake assessment. The nursing aide came to our house. We sat right here in this kitchen and set up a schedule that Mom agreed to!"

"Girls, can you please not argue?" my mother called out from the family room.

I cut to the pocket door and closed it, returning to face my sister.

"The decision was made," I said. "Why didn't you stick up for me?"

My sister stared at me like I had three heads. "I don't see the problem."

"Because it doesn't affect you."

"Well, you're not working," said my sister.

She didn't just say that, I thought.

"Taking care of Mom *is* a full time job," I said, infuriated. "That's why I don't have time for a normal job—and never will until I get some help here."

"Well… I can help you on the weekends," said my sister. "I'll take Mom to the salon when she needs her hair done, and take her to her nail appointments."

"Sure… okay." There was no point in arguing. My sister didn't get it. Or if she did, she wasn't bothered by my predicament, which was a truly painful thought.

Feeling totally blindsided, I went into the family room.

"Why did you change your mind?" I said to my mother, lying on the couch.

She opened her eyes, confused.

"About the home health aide worker," I added.

She closed her eyes. "I don't want a stranger coming to the house."

"The intake specialist was a stranger, and she came to our house."

"That was different," said my mother.

"But you agreed—"

She cut me off. "I don't want to talk about it."

My head felt like it was about to explode.

I went upstairs, needing to put some physical distance between my mother and myself. Inside the renovated den, I closed the door and sat at the long, black desk. I stared out the window, at the ice-hardened branches of a magnolia tree on the other side of the glass. The stillness of everything around me seemed to focus my mind. I resolved to revisit the issue of the home health aide worker at some point in the New Year. For now I had to find a workaround.

I had an idea: put an ad on Craigslist and get a driver for Mom. I could pay someone fifteen or twenty dollars per hour to at least take her to her physical therapy appointments. I drew up the ad and posted it that night, doing an end-run around everyone.

TWO MONTHS LATER, I was visiting my sister Zoë in Florida—alone, while my mother stayed in DC with her sister—when I received an e-mail with the words "Foreign Service Officer Selection Process Results" in the subject line. I averted my eyes from the computer. Finally, I downloaded the attached PDF letter, reading it in astonishment.

I had not been invited to participate in the Oral Assessment, the next stage of my Foreign Service application. There was no explanation as to why I'd been rejected, and I would never learn why, because applicants are not told who reviews a file or why a decision is made. I just sat there staring at the computer screen. Why had I even bothered to go to graduate school? Thousands of dollars in tuition, countless papers on diplomacy, endless group projects, and here I wasn't even given a chance to interview for a position in my field.

Tears filled my eyes. *It's over*, I thought. *They don't want me.* In the results letter, I was encouraged to reapply. But that meant starting from scratch: taking the exam again, waiting for the results, writing the essays, getting recommendations, and more weeks of waiting. *No way*, I thought, hurt and angry. But I knew the Foreign Service wasn't for me. Not anymore.

My ego had been bruised, but after a few moments, I began to feel lighter. Because now it was clear that I wouldn't be going overseas, which meant I didn't have to leave my mother. And I didn't want to leave her, no matter how demanding the past year had been. I wanted to move out and be on my own, but I didn't have to go overseas to accomplish that. But what would I do next?

WHEN I GOT BACK TO Maryland, I began exploring my work options, hastily, because as much as I loved my mother, the thought of living indefinitely with her in suburbia felt like joining a cult. I had to find a way out. I told myself I could teach or produce short documentary pieces for the World Bank, where a friend worked freelance. Combing the Internet, I researched organizations and job openings. I went to a K-8 Progressive Schools job fair, met with my World

Bank contact, and paid visits to the Center For American Progress.

Nothing panned out.

As the days wore on, I felt like I was decomposing spiritually. I craved my freedom, but was bound by my impoverishment and the fear of separating from my mother, who needed attention of one sort or another. My stealth Craigslist ad had produced a driver for my mother, which freed up some of my time, but I still had to wake my mother up every morning to keep her from sleeping until noon or later, remind her to take her pills, and accompany her to appointments. Working from home was the best option.

An idea came to me one day, as I was sitting in the den, staring out the window at our backyard. It was early spring and the dogwood was in full bloom, splashing white across the green hillside. By now my father had been gone from our lives for well over a year. I felt less mournful than in the past, but I was more restless than ever.

It occurred to me that my mother probably never wanted to write the White House volunteer book in the first place—that she liked the idea of the book more than the actual process of writing it. The impulse to pen her note at 4 a.m. was the same impulse that had set in motion our ill-advised trip to Milan. But maybe my mother had unknowingly raised the idea of writing the book to spark a creative fire in me. I thought, *I'm supposed to be writing my own book, not hers.* It was terrifying to know this was what I should do, and that the decision had been made. But it was also exhilarating. I thought, *as long as I'm living here, why shouldn't I try?*

I backed into writing this book after pursuing dozens of jobs for which I was completely ill-suited, and after coming to the realization that I had been given the gift of time to fulfill a lifelong ambition. At the same time, I realized that as long as I remained in the house, I would have to continue looking after my mother. Everything came with a price tag.

IN THE MONTHS that followed, I became lost in the ebb and flow of a life led in increments. I gave up on the idea of predicting when we would sell the house. But I knew it was the only real escape hatch I had left. For estate planning reasons, the property had been transferred to my sisters and me, which meant the three of us owned it. The mortgage was paid off, and my mother was comfortable enough financially to let the proceeds from the sale of the house be divided among us daughters. With my share of the proceeds, I could continue writing and developing my career without worrying about money for a year or two.

The problem was, my mother wasn't ready to let go of the house, and her desire to stay in it trumped any argument I could make about why she should move out. So I grew more anxious by the day. But in June—eighteen months after my father's death—my mother caved in on another front, agreeing to let me hire a home health aide. This tempered my anxiety, ever so slightly.

In the meantime, having come to the conclusion that my mother's neurologist was either withholding information or utterly clueless, I took her to a specialist at the Johns Hopkins Bayview Medical Center in Baltimore. I felt relieved, as if I were finally in expert hands. But when the doctor sat down with me alone and told me he thought my mother was in the early stages of Alzheimer's disease, I began crying silent tears.

I shouldn't have been surprised, but hearing the diagnosis after months of speculation came as a shock. But I had observed some of the classic symptoms firsthand, and my mother's second in-depth cognitive test, conducted a year after the first one, confirmed the same signs, such as having difficulty speaking at times, finding the right word, and not always knowing what day it was.

"Let's bring your mother in," said the doctor. "Can I use the 'A' word with her?"

I nodded, saying, "She can handle it."

My mother came into the room. When the doctor gave his diagnosis, her face went rigid.

"Well, I guess I'll just have to get used to it," she said.

I wasn't convinced the label "Alzheimer's" applied to my mother. Maybe I was in denial, but I knew the spectrum of dementia was broad, and that Alzheimer's could only be definitively diagnosed after examining the brain at death. I wasn't eager for that definitive diagnosis, so I just continued to do what I was doing: preserving my mother's quality of life.

But as time went on, living in our family home began to feel like living in a mausoleum. My father was everywhere. Not just in photographs, but also in the curly handwriting of his fuse box labels, the tobacco smell of his cigar case, and even the barbecue grill he assembled. The house no longer felt like my home. It was a place for me to sleep and a repository for my mother's memories. I was desperate to know when we would be leaving.

And then one day, I came into the kitchen to find that my mother hadn't emptied the dishwasher as promised. I almost fainted in distress. But instead of picking a fight with my mother, I shot to my bedroom and called my sister Tasha.

"I can't do this anymore," I said, my body shaking as I began sobbing, explaining what had happened. "There has to be an ending."

"I understand," said my sister. "But we have to do what's best for Mom."

"But it's not fair to *me*." I clamped the phone to my ear. "I've been here for two years—taking care of Mom, the house and trying to rebuild my life. I can hold out a little longer, as long as I know there's a plan in place. But we need to sell the house."

"Well," my sister said, "maybe it's time."

"It's *definitely* time." I paused. "I can start decluttering now, and we can put the house on the market in November."

"Okay," said Tasha, softening. "Maybe it's for the best."

I called Zoë afterward, and she agreed it was time to sell. Then I broached the topic with my mother.

"We have to sell the house," I said, at dinner that night. "It's not going to happen tomorrow, but now we have a timeline."

"I guess it's inevitable," said my mother, her shoulders slumping. "But where will I live?"

"Where do you want to live?" I said. "Other than here."

"With you."

I let out a sigh. "Mom, I love you… but we can't live together."

"You want your life back," she said, with a knowing smile. "I understand."

It was then that I realized her therapy sessions were helping.

I BEGAN DECLUTTERING the house, and investigating alternate living situations for my mother. Part of me resented having to do this, but I knew nothing would happen unless I took charge of the process. In the end, my mother decided to move in with my aunt, who lived in a four-story townhouse in DC. This solution proved to be disastrous, but an indispensible stepping-stone for where my mother later wound up: a retirement home in Georgetown.

During the time I prepared the house for sale, my mother visited Zoë in Florida. As I pulled out of the driveway to take her to the airport, she said goodbye to the house where she had raised us and lived with Dad. My mother never looked back. Months later, she told me she didn't remember much about the first year after my father's death, or about our years in the house without him. She said that at times she had a sensation of the time period, as if it were a phantom limb lingering in the corners of her mind, but she didn't remember her day-to-day emotions.

I remembered mine vividly, because I was awake for more hours and paying attention for both of us. It was the hardest time of my life, but also the most rewarding, because it gave my life meaning beyond anything I was striving for professionally. I realized my happiest moments were when I was helping my mother. There was no substitute for the satisfaction I felt providing her with the same unwavering strength that she had given to me in my childhood. And in an unexpected twist,

I found that caring for my mother allowed me to experience the motherhood I never had, with all of its ups and downs and hair-raising surprises. Like most new moms, I got better at it over time. And I knew that as long as my mother was alive, I would remain in the DC area. I couldn't and wouldn't leave her. What began as a temporary move had turned into something much more permanent.

Alone in our empty house, I supervised the presale renovations, sleeping on the only piece of furniture left: a day bed. Every now and then I became teary-eyed as I witnessed my childhood home transform into an impersonal piece of property being refurbished for the next owner. The process was slow and strange, but it was also therapeutic, allowing me to let go of my memories in a natural way. Our family had lived in the house for forty-two years.

On one of my last days there, I glanced out a spotless window, and froze up, stunned. The realtor had arranged for a For Sale sign to be placed on our property, and someone had come by and posted it when I wasn't paying attention. The sign was planted at the edge of the front lawn, near the curb of the cul-de-sac. I went outside and crept toward the For Sale sign as if it were a mirage. I stared at it for a moment, and then returned inside the house.

I sat down in the foyer, at the bottom of the stairs I had run up and down as a child. I put my head in my hands and began crying. It was time to leave.

Acknowledgments

MANY PEOPLE HAVE HELPED in the creation of this book, but none more than my editor, Barbara Esstman. Thank you for challenging me to dig deeper and do better, for your wit and words of praise, and for dragging me over the finish line before I collapsed. I am grateful to have found you, Barbara. You're the real deal.

Thanks also to Patty Housman for reading early drafts, providing feedback, and checking in on my progress even as the manuscript languished. Immense gratitude to Glen Finland for encouraging me to "keep slugging along," and to Rashid Darden, Elizabeth Collins, Mark Harris and Nancy Lloyd, for providing nuggets of wisdom that kept me focused and sane.

Thanks to Michele and Ronda at 1106 Design, the team that built this book and held my hand as I leapt into the unknown world of self-publishing. And to their wonderful colleague: copy editor Laura Bowley, who cleaned up my linguistic messes, and alerted me to the ongoing war between "further" and "farther."

I am grateful to friends and family members, near and far, for their unwavering support. Huge hugs to my sisters Tasha and Zoë, who stopped asking "how's the book coming?" long ago, and quietly kept the faith.

To my incredible parents, who I adore beyond words and will look up to even when I hit ninety: thank you for being the net beneath my lifelong high-wire act. I am one lucky gal to have grown up under your roof.

Finally, special thanks to my mother, Helen—my champion, partner in crime, fellow wordsmith and impish delight—for taking me on a journey I will always cherish, and never forget. Most of all, thank you for your courageous reply when I said you might not like some of the things I wrote about you in this book. "It's the truth, isn't it?" she said. Priceless, and vintage Mom.

www.ingramcontent.com/pod-product-compliance
Lightning Source LLC
Chambersburg PA
CBHW020609300426
44113CB00007B/563